THE LIBRARY
OF
THE UNIVERSITY
OF CALIFORNIA
LOS ANGELES

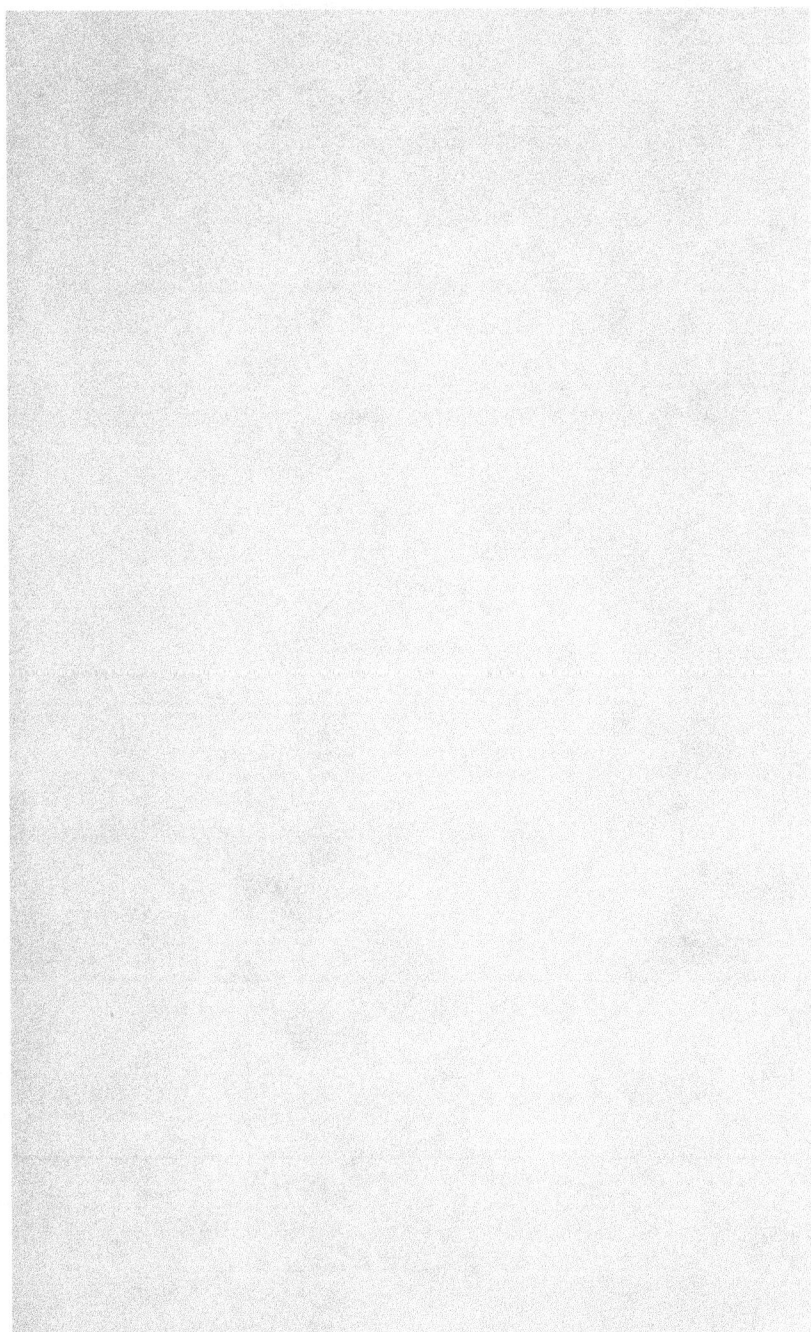

First Published April, 1921.

SOCIALISM AND CO-OPERATION

By

LEONARD S. WOOLF

THE NATIONAL LABOUR PRESS, LTD.

LONDON AND MANCHESTER

— 1921 —

CONTENTS.

Socialism and Co-operation.

CHAPTER I.

THE FOUNDATIONS OF SOCIALISM.

THE object of this book is to examine the relations between co-operation and socialism, to determine, if possible, the part which the co-operative system might play in a socialistic society. By co-operation I mean the consumer's type of co-operation which has developed in the distributive and wholesale societies of the existing co-operative movement. In these pages I shall assume generally that the reader knows how that movement is constituted and organized and that he understands the principle underlying the co-operative system of industry. I have already in another book, *Co-operation and the Future of Industry*, given a general description of the movement and of its characteristics as an industrial system, and I must refer to that book any reader who desires detailed information on or discussion of those points. While, however, I do not propose to give a detailed description either of co-operation or of socialism, it is impossible to arrive at a clear understanding of the relations between them, unless we have first stated clearly what we mean by co-operation and what we mean by socialism. In this chapter I shall attempt to clear the ground by defining socialism and co-operation.

It is far easier to define co-operation than socialism. The former is merely a particular method or system of conducting industry which we can already see working within certain limits in the retail and whole-sale societies. Socialism is an ideal or theory applicable to the whole of society. The socialist wants the whole of society, not merely the industrial section of it, to be organized in a particular manner; he wants a socialistic society. Socialism is therefore a much wider and larger thing than co-operation, and the wider a conception is the more difficult it is to keep it clear-cut and defined in our minds. The difficulty is increased in the case of socialism by its history. For a hundred years, if not longer, it has remained an ideal or aspiration of thinkers, writers, and workers who are in revolt against the existing organization of society. Until three years ago every socialist would have agreed that society had never and nowhere actually been organized on socialist principles. An ideal, aspiration, or theory concerning so complex a thing as the whole organization of society is necessarily unstable. The original theory or ideal may have been as precise and as lucid as the ten commandments which the Almighty cut in stone and gave to Moses, but, as it is handed down from generation to generation and is never made concrete by actual application or experiment, it becomes covered by the accretions of the theories of new writers and the ideals, hopes, or despairs of new generations.

This is what has happened to socialism, and to-day it is extremely difficult to say what socialism is or who is and who is not a socialist. Robert Owen is a socialist, and so are Karl Marx, and Mr. Ramsay MacDonald, and Lenin, and Mr. Cole, and M. Longuet, and Mr.

Smillie, and Trotsky, and Mr. Sidney Webb. I have
called each of these gentlemen a socialist, because
each would call himself a socialist. I believe in
freedom of thought, and it seems to me absurd to
forbid anyone to think and call himself a socialist if
he wishes to do so. It is, however, notorious that
Lenin and Trotsky would deny that many of the others
mentioned were socialists, while some of the others
would deny that Lenin and Trotsky's system of society
had any right to call itself socialism.

It is essential that a writer on socialism should face
this difficulty and make his position clear at the outset.
I am aware that, although I call myself and think
myself a socialist, many other socialists will deny that
what I call socialism is really socialism. I cannot
return the compliment. I believe that most people who
honestly consider themselves to be socialists are such.
Lenin and Mr. Sidney Webb are both socialists,
because they both wish the foundations of social
organization to be of a certain kind. They may differ
fundamentally on other, and possibly equally important, questions, on, e.g., the means by which the
social revolution may be attained, but they do agree
on this vital point : they wish to substitute a socialistic
for a capitalistic society.

It may be thought that in the last sentence I have
only carried the disagreement between these so-called
socialists a step further back. For what after all is
a " socialistic society " ? Will not Lenin on this point
disagree as fundamentally with Mr. Webb as he does
with Lord Northcliffe? But as soon as the question
is put in that way, it becomes apparent that there
is a fundamental basis of agreement among all these
so-called socialists. At the bottom of Lenin's heart

or brain is a drop of Fabianism, and all Mr. Webb's
cleverness cannot conceal his Bolshevism.   On the
other hand, however deep you might delve in the
mind of Lord Northcliffe, you would never find this
little drop of Fabianism and Bolshevism, this kernel
of agreement between Lenin and Mr. Sidney Webb.
It is this kernel of agreement which I call socialism
and which I now propose to define.

Society as we know it in the civilized States of
Western Europe is organized capitalistically. Capitalistic society is based upon the division of the population into well defined classes.   There is a land-
owning class, a capital-owning class, a professional
class with or without capital, and a property-less
wage-earning class.   The existence and continuance
of these classes, and the whole organization of
capitalist society, depend ultimately upon the law of
private property.   The land-owning and capitalist
classes, which are a small minority of the community,
own and control practically all the land and capital
in the country, and the law and therefore the whole
power of the State is used to maintain their
monopoly.   This is, of course, the barest possible
sketch of the organization of a capitalist society, and
it is essential that both socialists and those who are
considering the nature of socialism should understand
the real nature of the organization and the causes
which produce it.   The reason is this.   Most people
are inclined to divide the world into sheep and goats,
the sheep being the good who agree, and the goats
the bad who disagree with them.   This fatal inclina-
tion vitiates nine-tenths of political, economic, and
social theory and investigation.   The author of this
book is a socialist and co-operator, and he knows well

that ordinarily he finds it extremely hard not to
believe that the socialist and co-operator are good and
the capitalist bad. But when he faces the confessional
of the virgin sheet of paper upon which he must begin
to write the first chapter of his book, he knows that
this belief is false. Capitalism is bad and socialism
is good, but capitalists are not bad, nor socialists good.
The truth is that there is very little average difference
in the goodness and badness of the various sects of
men; the fundamental difference in men from the
political and social point of view will be found in
their beliefs and in their desires. Capitalists believe
certain things about society which are false and
desire certain things in society which are bad; socialists believe certain things about society which are true
and desire certain things in society which are good.
That is the real difference between them, and it is
doubtful whether it makes the average socialist a
better man than the average capitalist.

I believe the point which I am trying to make in
the previous paragraph to be of the first importance
for the political or social writer and student, but I
am aware that as stated here it is not entirely clear
and probably not completely correct. Perhaps I may
make my meaning clearer by an actual example.
When I read the *Times* and *Morning Post*, and when
I speak to upholders of the capitalist system, I find
that they are genuinely convinced that Lenin and
Trotsky are not only men who have wrong beliefs
on politics and social organization, but also are
desperately wicked men. Again, when I read the
Daily Herald, or speak to socialists, or look into my
own mind, I find that we not only believe that Mr.
Churchill and Lord Northcliffe are men who hold false

beliefs with regard to politics and social organization, but also that they are abominably bad men. At the same time, to put it mildly, the capitalist and his press regard Mr. Churchill and we and our press regard Lenin as good men beyond the average. Now wherever this kind of situation arises, where there is a dogmatic co-ordination between one's beliefs and moral judgments, it should, I think, be regarded with the gravest suspicion. At one time it was accepted universally with regard to religious beliefs, but the world has moved forward sufficiently for most people now to see clearly that a man who believes in Muhammadanism is not necessarily better than a man who believes in Christianity or *vice versa*, and that a Roman Catholic is not necessarily a better man than an Anglican or *vice versa*.

I am not going to apologize for spending so much time over this point at the beginning of a short book upon social organization, for it goes to the root of the attitude which we are to adopt towards the study of contemporary society. What vitiates the work of so many writers on politics, economics, and sociology is that they are not so much concerned with investigating the effects of various forms of social organization, the effects of men's communal beliefs and desires upon society and man in society, as with investigating the moral badness of the system which they dislike and of the supporters of that system with whom they disagree. The truth of the matter appears to me to be something like this. It is true that a belief in capitalism implies one series of social beliefs and desires, and a belief in socialism implies another and a different series. The capitalist believes that one kind of social organization is the right one and he desires certain things in society produced by that kind of organization; the socialist believes that a completely different organization is the right one and he desires different things to be produced by this organization. Both the capitalist and the socialist believe that the ultimate things which they desire in society are good and that particular forms of social organization will produce these things. Now it is certainly of the utmost importance to discover whether the things desired by the socialists or those desired by the capitalists are good, and it is true that, if what the socialist desires as good is really good and what the capitalist desires as good is really bad, or *vice versa*, then the socialist is a better man than the capitalist, or *vice versa*. It is also extremely important to discover whether the forms of organization, etc., which each believes are means to the good things which they desire, do or do not produce those things.

It follows that the less a writer or student concerns himself with moral judgments on sects and classes of persons, and particularly on the classes of those who politically agree or disagree with him, the more likely he is to keep his eyes clear and his head steady on the treacherous and slippery paths of social science. Our main business is not with capitalists or socialists and their goodness and badness, but with the beliefs and desires of capitalism and socialism. We have to find out what those things are which capitalists and socialists desire, and whether the things desired by them are good or bad in themselves. We also have to find out whether the beliefs of capitalists and socialists that certain forms of social organization will produce these social goods and bads are true or false. It is not only for these reasons that it is essential to determine at the outset what are the ultimate social aims and beliefs of capitalists and socialists, but also because it is the acceptance or rejection of them by the majority of living men and women which produces the form of society in which those men and women live.

Let us first, before we pass on to the ideal of socialists, examine a little more closely the actuality of capitalism. Capitalism, though the product and ideal of practical business men, is based upon a curious paradox. The capitalist undoubtedly believes that his ultimate social aim or desire is the highest good of the whole community. " What I desire," he would say, " from social organization is that it should work in the interests not of individuals and classes, but of the whole community." And remembering what we said with regard to the goodness and badness of those sects of men with whom we disagree, let us admit that this ultimate desire exists and is really operative in the capitalist and his society. In fact, if this were not the case, the centrifugal forces in capitalist society would long since have utterly destroyed it. The capitalist only exists and has been able to maintain his precarious but disastrous existence in the world by being, at the bottom of his heart, a socialist, and by accepting at the back of his mind the beliefs of socialism. But the paradox of capitalism consists in this : that, while recognizing that the interests of the whole community, not of classes or individuals, should be the ultimate end of social organization, the capitalist goes on to announce the amazing dogma that the interests of the whole community rather than of individuals and classes can only be secured by organizing society in the interests of individuals and

classes. The capitalist arrives at his present position
in which he accepts this paradox, as automatically
and undoubtingly as our forefathers accepted the
statement that the earth is flat, through a series of
beliefs which, in my opinion and those of other
socialists, are false. He believes, for instance, that
the good of the whole community can only be secured
by encouraging individuals and classes to devote their
lives to a ruthless pursuit of their own interests. He
believes that society should be so organized as to
give free play to the competition of class against class,
and individual against individual, for a share in the
material, intellectual, æsthetic, and even moral products of society. He believes—and this is his one
correct belief—that this system of competition can
only be maintained on the legal institution of private
property in land and other material commodities, a
system under which the whole power of the community
is used to protect the individual in his possession of
such material things as he has contrived to snatch
according to the rules of the game from the community
of his fellow-men. He believes that the good of the
whole community can only be secured if the income
of the community is distributed so that the maximum
amount is given to a tiny minority and the minimum
to the vast majority of the community. He believes
that the good of the whole community can only be
secured if those who are born into the tiny class
possessing wealth are educated so that they can enjoy
the blessings of wealth and leisure, while those who
are born into the large class not possessed of property
are educated so that they can enjoy the blessings of
poverty and manual labour. He believes generally
that the good of the whole community can only be

secured if the control not only of industry but of
government is assured to the small class of property
owners and the parasites of property owners, and that
the right and democratic method of assuring this is
so to organize society that all the key positions of
control in the government of the country, the throne,
the cabinet, the ministers, the higher Civil Service,
the Benches of Judges and Magistrates, the Army and
Navy, and the Church, are occupied by property
owners or their parasites. Finally, the capitalist
usually believes that the good of the whole community
demands that the Press should be controlled by
capitalists and in the interests of capitalists, and that
a newspaper controlled by Labour and in the interests
of the majority of the community, is, if its circulation
exceeds 100, a menace to the safety of society.

These are the beliefs which are held implicitly in
a capitalist society by nearly all who accept or are
in sympathy with its methods and organization. They
are indeed held so implicitly and unconsciously that
most capitalists would angrily deny that they hold
them, for nothing is so irritating as to have our
unconscious beliefs rudely dragged to the surface of
our minds. The most serious charge against capitalism is, perhaps, not that it is based upon these false
unconscious beliefs, but rather that they produce
states of mind in individuals and classes which con-
taminate and rot the whole fabric of society. It is
at this point that, in my opinion, is to be found
the fundamental difference between capitalism and
socialism, and it is therefore important to make this
charge against capitalism perfectly clear; otherwise
much that I shall have to say about a socialist society
in the latter part of this book will not be fully under-

stood. Capitalism is founded, we saw, upon the
paradox that the ultimate end of social organization
is the good of the whole community, but that the
good of the whole community can only be attained
by organizing society in classes so that each individual
and each class pursues, not the good of the community, but his own or its own interest. The result
is that the whole of society becomes immediately
permeated by the principle of competition and self-
interest. The community of fellow-citizens is transformed into a mass of struggling units in which the
possessors are compelled to fight blindly to retain
what they possess, while the only aim of those who
do not possess is to oust the possessors. Everywhere
the desires for the selfish interests of individuals and
classes, rather than of the community, sets and keeps
in motion the machinery and the life of society. In
the economic sphere every individual is taught from
his earliest years that the main business of his life
is to " make a living " for himself, to try to get as
much of the economic product of society as he can
for himself, and to prevent as much as he can from
going into the pockets of his neighbours. The
capitalist, in the pursuit of his own profits, will
defraud the State, ruin his fellow-capitalist, and join
with his fellow-capitalist to exploit the worker and
consumer, while the worker, in his struggle for wages,
again and again finds that in order to protect his
own interests he has to sacrifice those of his fellow-
workers or of the whole commmunity. But this
extraordinary system of organizing society in the
interests of the whole community cannot be confined
merely to the economic sphere. It flows over into
and contaminates every other sphere of life, govern-

ment, art, sport, religion, leisure, even love and
marriage. In the politics and government of civilized
countries no pretence any longer is made that the
good of the whole community is a serious consideration for parties and politicians. The political stage
is set for a struggle between two or more great political
machines, or parties, each pursuing its own interests.
Its interests consist in power and office, and it obtains
these by several different means, by deceiving the
ignorant elector, by corruption open or secret, by
selling honours, by doles or bribes to organized labour,
and by breaking any politician who may show signs
of independence. Individuals, therefore, in a capitalist society enter politics merely in order to get
something out of them, while government and political
power have become little more than instruments in
the struggle between individuals and classes.

Politics and government are necessarily so closely
connected with the economic life and organization of
a community that the inter-effect of one upon the
other is inevitable. But so powerful and penetrating
are the beliefs and desires of capitalism, the effects
of inculcating self-interest and profit-making into the
individual as the proper motive of his actions during
six-sevenths of his waking life, that they infect those
corners of the community which theoretically should
be absolutely free from them. Two illuminating
examples may be given. We are expected to believe
that if anywhere in society something is pursued for
its own sake and not for material profits, it is in art,
literature, philosophy, and science. Art for art's sake
and truth for truth's sake are still represented as the
objects of the artist, the writer, or the scientist. But
during the 100 or 150 years of industrialized capit-

alism, art, literature, and science have been so thoroughly commercialized and industrialized that their peculiar ideals have been either destroyed or perverted. No age in European history can compare with our own in the enormous quantity and the worthless quality of pictures painted and books written. One reason is that the artist, writer, or scientist is part of the capitalist machine, and, if he does not conform to the rhythm of its revolutions, he will be broken. The production and distribution of pictures and books, for instance, tends more and more to become a particular province of large-scale capitalist enterprise, and people read books and consider them masterpieces, just as they take patent pills and consider that they cure backache, because the advertisement tells them to. No one without a knowledge of the trade would imagine how difficult it would be to-day to get a book even produced which did not conform to the standards of commercialized and industrialized literature, and, even if it were printed, a far smaller number of persons (out of a population of millions) would probably read it than in other non-capitalist ages, such as ancient Greece, though the population was numbered only in thousands, consumed and appreciated a similar work of art. Most writers and artists are therefore faced with the alternative of either writing or painting for the capitalist machine, i.e., to make a profit, or of starving. That is certainly not true of ancient Greece, the Elizabethan age, the eighteenth century, or even the first part of the nineteenth century, and the effect can, in my opinion, be traced not only in the different attitude of the artist and writer in those ages towards their work, but also in the quality of their productions.

But the mechanical effect of capitalist organization
is not the most important influence of capitalism upon
art and literature. The author of this book must here
be allowed to speak from personal experience, and
his personal experience would compel him to confess
that it is quite impossible for a writer to escape being
permeated by capitalist ideals. So subtly pervading
is the mental environment, the beliefs and desires,
of the society in which one lives, that, however
strongly one may intellectually disapprove of them,
they again and again, unobserved, mould one's own
beliefs and desires and determine one's own actions.
Quite apart from the mechanical exigencies of
publishers, printers, and booksellers, no writer can
say that his literary or professional conscience is
untouched by the profit-making complex of capitalist
society. This book is, for instance, written in, I
believe, the honest conviction that capitalism is bad
just because it creates and fosters this profit-making
complex, this universal itch to be making something
out of everything ; yet the book would probably never
have been written, and even this page would probably
have been written differently, had not the author
nursed a, certainly hopeless, hope that he would make
something out of it.

What I have said with regard to the author and
artist applies with even greater force to the scientist,
and the civilized capitalist ought somehow to explain
the undoubted fact that all the great scientific discoveries of the last hundred years have contributed
more to the sum of human misery than to the sum
of human happiness. But the most startling evidence
of the effect of capitalist organization and ideals is
to be found in the sphere of labour and socialism.

Probably nine out of ten socialists are genuine
believers in socialism ; they see the evils of the capitalist system and honestly desire to abolish them and it.
Yet anyone with experience of the labour and socialist
movements, both national and international, will
admit that their greatest weakness lies in the fact
that they are unconsciously permeated by the beliefs
and desires of capitalism.   If, for instance, the
principle of social service really ousted the ideals of
profit-making and competition among individuals and
classes professing socialism, labour would only have
to blow with its trumpets and the walls of capitalism
would fall down as flat as those of Jericho.   That
this does not happen is due to the fact not only that
the individuals who compose labour and socialist
movements are forced to struggle for existence in a
world of capitalism, but that from their earliest years
their minds are necessarily and unconsciously satur-
ated with the individualist, competitive, and profit-
making capitalist conceptions and ideals.   The
socialist, like the writer, is perverted and corrupted
by his environment.   It is not his fault, but it is none
the less a fact in existing society which the socialist
who desires radical change must face, and which the
social philosopher must recognize and estimate as one
of the products of capitalism.   Over and over again
in the trade union or syndicalist movements,
economic action against capitalism breaks down owing
to what is called a " lack of solidarity."   Translate
this euphemism into plain English and you find that,
just as the writer is pursuing his own interest and
profit instead of " art " or " truth," so the worker
is pursuing not a social end, but the immediate
interest or profit of himself or his group against other

individuals or groups within his own class. In strikes, and indeed the whole relation of capital and labour, the exploitation of this capitalism of labour is the strongest weapon of the capitalist. In the co-operative movement, a great system of industry built up by the workers on principles and ideals utterly antagonistic to those of capitalism, there is always the same tendency operating strongly, playing upon the profit-making instincts of its members, perverting, weakening, and hampering the development of co-operative industry. But it is, perhaps, in the parliamentary labour and socialist movements and in the international labour and socialist movements that the effect of a capitalist environment has been most strong and most disastrous. Up to the war the failure of the parliamentary movement in all countries was obvious; it was due partly to the fact that capitalist principles and ideals had a stronger appeal to and a firmer hold upon the rank and file of workers than those of labour and socialism; but everyone who has studied the history of this movement in France, Germany, and Britain during the last generation will agree that no small part of its weakness has come from the ease with which the capitalist machine of government has been able to exploit the anti-socialistic instincts within the parliamentary socialist parties. As for the international movement, the war showed clearly to what an extent it had been permeated with the beliefs and desires of its capitalist environment.

I repeat that in this analysis I am concerned neither with praise nor with blame. Socialists, and I among them, start with the postulate that the modern world is sick of a mortal social disease. Our diagnosis or analysis is a preliminary to the discovery of a cure.

But the diagnosis, if it is to be of any use, must be ruthless to the patient, and particularly to that part of the patient which consists of ourselves. Capitalism will never be destroyed by throwing stones at capitalists and by pocketing the coins which the capitalists skilfully mix with the stones which they throw at us. If we are to cure society we must understand exactly the nature of its disease and the manner in which and the extent to which it has permeated individuals and classes. I am not concerned to praise or blame the socialist writer who is out to make a profit, or the socialist leader who accepts a well-paid post in some capitalist Government or is carried away by the patriotism of capitalism to support imperialist wars to end wars; but, as a writer on socialism and co-operation who wishes to see capitalism make way for something better, I am very much concerned with noting the existence and effects of these significant phenomena.

This analysis of the social philosophy of capitalism and of its effects has been long, but its utility will, I hope, become apparent now that we have to examine the alternative presented by socialism. The socialist begins by denying the paradox of capitalism; he denies that, if you want to make the ultimate end of social organization the interests not of classes or individuals but of the whole community, you should make the competitive interests of individuals and classes the basis of your social organization. The common interests of the community will never be attained by the whole of society, if they are deliberately excluded from the several parts of society and from the everyday life of individuals and classes. To organize society on the basis of competition

between individuals and classes, and to encourage
individuals and classes to pursue only their material
advantage and profit, inevitably has two results : the
common good or communal interests cease in practice
to become a motive of action, while individuals or
classes which have been clever, cunning, or lucky
enough to do well for themselves in the struggle for
power and profit will establish themselves in so strong
a position of privilege and vested interest that they
will be able to make the whole machinery of society
work, not for the common good of society, but for
the preservation and extension of their own
monopolies and interests.   No, argues the socialist,
in human affairs if you aim at producing Z, it is neither
usual nor reasonable to concentrate your whole atten-
tion upon producing A.   A farmer, whose ultimate
end is the production of a field of corn in August,
does not usually sow his field with tares in the spring.
If the ultimate end of social organization be the
common interests of the members of society, then we
should organize society so that in every part of it the
common interests, not the separate interests of
individuals and classes, are the visible aim of the
organization, and so that the motives of individual
action are not selfish but social.

The task which the socialist thus sets himself in
revolutionizing society is far more formidable than
he sometimes seems to realize. He has, in the first
place, to devise an organization which, both as a whole
and in its several parts, is based upon communal
interests. He has to show that such an organization
will work and will, in fact, produce the results which
it is intended to produce. But even that is not
enough ; he has also to show that, given his particular

rearrangement of the social organization, individuals
and classes will accept communal interests as the
motives of their social actions. It is the bearing of
the co-operative principles of industry upon these
formidable problems of socialism which I propose to
examine in the following pages.

First let us attempt to define what may be called
the postulates of socialism, those postulates which all
socialists accept and of which the acceptance distinguishes the socialist from the capitalist. They exist
and are of importance. The socialist, as we have seen,
starts from the position that society should be
organized as a whole and in its several parts for the
benefit of all, and that this cannot be attained if the
basis of political or economic organization, for
instance, is competition between classes or individuals
for their own interests or for profit. So far as the
mere machinery of organization is concerned, therefore, socialism must strike at the root of the capitalist
principle which economically organizes society on a
basis of competition between classes and individuals.
The root of competition and therefore of capitalism
is the private ownership of the vital economic
resources of the community. So long as individuals
own, organize, and control land and capital, the competitive system must dominate society, for every
individual or class is compelled to take part in a ceaseless struggle against other individuals or classes for
the ownership or control of the means of production
or the commodities produced.

Here we find the justification for the enormous
importance assigned by socialism to the economic
factor in the organization of modern society. If the
private ownership and control of the economic

resources is recognized in a highly industrialized
community such as that of Britain in the 19th century
and is protected by the whole power of the modern
State, the internecine struggle—a struggle which at
one end of the scale is a struggle for profits, and at
the other a struggle for bare existence—must inevitably dominate the life of the individual, the class,
and the whole community. It is important to notice
that the social disease in the virulent form which is
attacked by socialism can only exist in a highly
industrialized and capitalistic society. Where, as
was the rule before the 19th century, the earth was
covered with thin and scattered agricultural and
pastoral communities, where men lived mainly upon
the land and obtained the commodities consumed by
them for the most part directly from the land under
their feet, the internecine struggle, as we know it,
scarcely existed : the struggle for existence was not
between individuals and classes, but against nature,
and, when men starved, they were starved not by
their fellow-men, but by the sun or the rain or the
hurricane. But to-day in London or Manchester no
man produces what he consumes, nor does the whole
community consume what it produces; every
individual is therefore part of an intricate economic
machine, and the right to control that machine or
any part of it becomes of enormous importance. At
one end of the scale an individual or class, by controlling the machine or part of it, can and does obtain
an inordinate share of the commodities produced ; at
the other end of the scale a man, with no control over
any part of the machinery, if he for one instant fails
to keep his position within the machine, will find himself deprived of the barest necessaries of existence.

Thus in the capitalistic industrialized State the individual is compelled to carry on a perpetual struggle, not against nature, but against his neighbour; and, when men starve, they are starved not by drought or flood, but by the elaborate stupidity of the social machinery which they have created, machinery which any intelligent ant or bee would be ashamed of, but which man himself proudly calls civilization.

These facts account for the stress laid by socialism upon the economic organization of society. The fundamental principle of socialism, the principle which distinguishes the socialist from the non-socialist, is the belief that the economic resources of the community should be owned and controlled not by individuals or by classes, but by the whole community. But the exact meaning or nature of this principle and belief must be clearly understood. Many opponents of socialism, and indeed many socialists themselves, completely misunderstand them. The communal ownership and control of the economic resources of the community are not an end in themselves. There is no reason to believe that the man without property is a better man than the man with property, or even that the England of to-day would be a better England if the mines were nationalized than if they were not nationalized. No, communal ownership can only be defended on the ground that, and if, it produces certain social conditions and a certain social psychology, while it destroys the evil social conditions and social psychology of capitalism. Socialism aims at communal ownership and control only because it believes that in that way alone the following conditions will be produced : the organization of society on the

basis of a struggle between individuals and classes
for their immediate profit, for monopolies or privileges,
or for bare existence, will be abolished; each part, as
well as the whole, of the machine of society will then
be enabled to work visibly for " the good of the whole
community," and not in the interests of particular
individuals or classes; the economic organization will
no longer create the economic psychology of capitalism; civilized men will no longer spend six-sevenths
of their lives in the curious occupation of trying to
buy in the cheapest and sell in the dearest market;
we shall cease to be dominated by the perpetual
necessity of pursuing material, selfish, and petty ends,
and the motives of our actions will be something a
little wider and even nobler than a 2s. rise in wages
or a profit of 25 per cent.

CHAPTER II.

SOCIALISM AND THE CONTROL OF INDUSTRY.

In the previous chapter I have examined the barest
foundations of socialism. I have tried to show that
the socialist aims at building up society on a basis
of co-operation between the units, whether individuals
or classes, of society and at making, therefore, not
competition or private profit, but communal interests
or communal service the visible end of social activities
in the every-day life of the individual. The condition
precedent to the existence of such a society is the
communal ownership and control of the economic
resources and instruments of the community.

But the socialist when he has arrived at this
position has only reached the fringe of his problem.
He has just succeeded in becoming aware that
he is a theoretical socialist rather than a theoretical
capitalist. Anyone with a little imagination can
construct in his mind's eye and—provided that
he can obtain a publisher—transfer to the pages
of a printed book an almost infinite series of societies
which would conform to our description of a socialist
society. For there are innumerable ways in which
the communal ownership of communal resources might
be organized and innumerable patterns into which the
units of society might be fitted so that, theoretically
at least, they spent their lives in harmony and co-
operation rather than in exploitation and competition.
That is why we have our Lenins and our Mr. Webbs,
our Christian Socialists, Social Democrats, Syndical-

c

ists, Guild Socialists, Communists; and that is why this chapter now has to be written.

I am afraid that I must trouble the reader to start from what is almost the alphabet of the subject and of his beliefs. But I shall do this of set purpose. Nothing is more salutary than to rethink one's elementary beliefs. Political stagnation and the impenetrable inertia of conservatism descend upon a man or society, when they accept any belief as so elementary as to be unquestionable. In science the greatest discoveries have been made by some perverse man who has questioned, rethought, and proved false the elementary truths of science. And what applies to science applies equally to politics and economics.

The problem which has produced the socialist and which he has to face is that of capitalistic industry. This is the fact that we must always have before our minds. It is the enormous, intricate machinery of production and distribution which dominates the lives of individuals and classes in modern western communities. The instruments and machinery of production and distribution include not only the factories and their plants, but the land and its minerals, etc., ships, railways, and other means of transport, the machinery of banking and finance, capital. Under the existing system the instruments and machinery are mainly in private hands and under private control. Wherever you examine this intricate machinery you find that society and its laws deliberately establish and protect private ownership, oligarchical control, and competition. The soil and its products, the subsoil and its products, the factories and machines, the banks, the ships, the railways, are in the hands and under the control of a minute minority of the population.

The whole individualist, capitalist system implies that the control is exercised in the interest and for the profit of the owners or controllers, and the implication is, in fact, fulfilled. Every step in the process of production and distribution is set in motion by the desire for private gain or profit. The farmer produces corn, the manufacturer makes cotton or iron goods, the baker bakes bread, the shipper runs his ships, the banker lends or borrows money, only if a profit can be made out of the transactions. And a profit can only be made if one can get hold of some part of the machine and gain control over a piece of soil or a factory or a ship or a bank. The instrument through which such control can be obtained is capital.

The task which the socialist sets himself is to re-organize this machinery of production and distribution. He has to establish communal instead of private-control over the machine, and to substitute communal for private ownership of economic resources and the instruments of production. His object, therefore, may be defined, from one point of view, as the democratization of industry. As soon as the problem is stated in this way, it will be seen that there are several alternative lines of organization open to the socialist. He may, for instance, take the community as a territorial unit, subdivided into other territorial units, and attempt to transfer the ownership of the economic resources and the instruments of production, and the ultimate control of industry, to these territorial units. The community is already organized geographically in the State, and geographical democracy when applied to industry inevitably issues in State socialism or Sovietism.

It was natural that the first impulse of the 19th

century socialist was to make the State and geographical democracy the basis of socialist organization.
He belonged to a generation which conceived high
hopes of political democracy; that new Leviathan, the
modern State, was just emerging, equipped with
tremendous powers for good or evil, from the slime
of the *ancien régime*; the future seemed to belong to
the democratic State. In these circumstances the rise
of social democracy or State socialism was inevitable.
It was so easy to identify the community with the
democratized State, and you had only to transfer the
ownership of land and the control of the economic
resources, the instruments of production, and industry
to the State, and you would bring the walls of capitalism tumbling down about the ears of its defenders
and at the same time raise upon its ruins the walls
of the socialist commonwealth. A passion for nationalization swept through the Labour and socialist movements, and Her Majesty's Postmaster General, as the
figure-head of the only nationalized industry, became
for many socialists the symbol of a new era.

These beliefs and theories have bitten so deep into
the Labour and socialist movements, particularly in
Britain, that their marks are clearly visible to-day.
Nationalization remains for many people a synonym
for socialism, and to hand over the mines or the
railways to a State department would in their opinion
mean a Red victory and a White defeat. I do not
propose here to enter very deeply into the question
of State socialism, since my reasons for rejecting it
will become apparent in my discussion of the co-
operative principle. But it is necessary to note briefly
the fact of and reasons for a widespread disillusionment in the ranks of the State socialists and nation-

alizers. The State is essentially the organ of political democracy and in the last thirty years both the State and political democracy have disappointed the majority of their most ardent supporters. The real cause of this phenomenon is rarely understood even by democrats and socialists, who are so occupied in finding in the evils of society stones which they may throw at their enemies that they neglect to enquire why the evils and the stones are there. The century which was brought to a characteristic and appropriate close by the great war and the Treaty of Versailles is chiefly remarkable for the failure of the 19th century conception of democracy. For democracy, as our fathers understood it, has not only failed to be democratic; it has refused to work. There are several States in the world to-day which, so far as the formal machinery of Government is concerned, are eminently " democratic." With their senates and chambers and referendums and universal suffrage they are admirably constructed political instruments upon which the people, had it the will and the skill, should be able to produce the highest democratic harmony. But the harmony is rarely, if ever, produced, and the instrument is used, not for expressing the will of a democracy, but for maintaining the power and promoting the interests of oligarchies. Government is actually carried on by little cliques, groups, or classes and by bureaucracies; the bureaucracies are firmly entrenched behind the politicians in the darkness of Government Offices above democratic control; the little political cliques and groups capture and maintain control of the complex machinery and power of the State by becoming the tool of class interests, by an elaborately organized system of private and public corruption,

and by a periodic debauch of lies and promises called
a general election.

Disillusionment not unnaturally has followed. The
State, which should be the organ and embodiment of
communal interests, is too obviously an engine of
exploitation and tyranny, while the institutions of
political democracy are used only either to give a
blank cheque to some oligarchy or to endorse its
actions and exactions. Practically everyone recognizes
and admits these facts and evils in countries or among
classes other than their own. Prussian militarism in
the form in which we crusaded against it was
admittedly only possible in a modern State under the
forms of a political democracy, and the Junker and
conscription were the corollaries of universal suffrage.
The socialist and the Bolshevik, too, are never tired
of analyzing the working of the bourgeois State and
the part which the representative Parliament and the
mechanism of political democracy have played in
fastening ever more securely the economic fetters
upon labour. But, while the disease which the British
patriot, the socialist, and the Bolshevik have observed
certainly exists, the observers have mistaken the
causes of its existence. The German and the capitalist,
and the natural wickedness of Germans and capitalists,
are not the cause of Prussian militarism and the
Prussian State, nor of the sham democracy of the
French and British bourgeois State. The real cause
is to be found in a political phenomenon closely allied
to the economic phenomenon with which I dealt briefly
in the previous chapter. Political democracy has
failed because the communal beliefs and desires
implied by it do not exist. A hundred and fifty years
ago a man or a small group of men could say : " I am

the State " or " We are the State," and not only did
the vast majority agree with them, but political
institutions and the machinery of government
accurately reflected this strange political belief. Men
believed in and desired oligarchy, and the oligarchical
society of the 18th century which was the result was,
with all its faults, alive, and it worked. But, as we
saw in the previous chapter, while communal beliefs
and desires produce particular forms of society, those
forms again tend to produce a particular form of social
psychology. The man who is born and bred in an
oligarchical society has the beliefs and desires implied
in oligarchy. The failure of 19th century democracy,
and the apotheosis of European civilization which we
have lived through between 1914 and 1921, are due to
the fact that, while the outer form or shell of 18th
century society was destroyed about 1789, its
communal psychology survived and survives. In the
last century there has been a slow, spasmodic transformation of social and political institutions, particularly the institutions of the State, from an oligarchic
to a democratic form. But there has been no corresponding transformation in the minds, in the communal
beliefs and desires of western communities. The
psychology of oligarchy and the psychology bred by
oligarchy remained when the Bastille had fallen and
Liberty, Equality, Fraternity had been proclaimed.
And the psychology of oligarchy is not confined to
the rulers and the ruling classes. The oligarchic mind
implies a belief, often unconscious, in the efficacy and
inevitability of rule from above, a desire either to rule
or to be ruled; it can only conceive society as a
hierarchy of classes and the main motive for action
as competition between individual and class interests.

The democratic mind, on the other hand, would imply
a belief in and a desire for co-operation in common
interests, a desire neither to rule nor to be ruled, but
to act together, as men often do in various forms of
sport, on an equality for a common end ; a desire to
express one's own individuality freely combined with
a very large tolerance of the free expression of their
individuality by other people ; and finally a conception
of society as composed not of competing individuals
and classes, but of citizens making individually or
collectively their distinctive contributions towards the
common life. This analysis has only to be stated in
order to show that the psychological conditions
necessary for the working of democratic institutions
have nowhere even begun to exist. Our psychology
remains oligarchic ; our rulers still desire to rule, while
the ruled, where they are not content to be ruled,
desire only to step into the shoes of the rulers ; the
tenacity with which the ruling and possessing classes
have fought to maintain their position of power and
privilege has forced the subject classes to see in
democracy and democratic institutions only weapons
for an intensified class warfare. In a word the
oligarchic mind which survived the 18th century has
corrupted the democracy of the 19th, so that the
pseudo-democracy of the 20th century breeds not
democrats but oligarchs.

These facts explain why it is the democrat who
is most dissatisfied with and most conscious of the
failure of the political democracy evolved by the last
century. To-day political democracy is inscribed on
the White banner of reaction and the Red Flag is
raised to the cry of " Down with political democracy."
A significant but not a surprising phenomenon. The

socialist, who agrees with the democrat and sees the impossibility of using the system and institutions of this pseudo-political democracy as the basis of communal ownership and control and industrial organization, is forced to consider alternative methods of organization. It is natural and reasonable that he should start from the existing organization of society and particularly of industry.

A survey of the modern community shows that, in the sphere of industry, its organization is based upon a sub-division into three great classes : a capitalist and land-owning class, a propertyless working class, and the consumers. (There are two other important classes of " producers " in the community, the autonomous practisers of a profession, such as the law, medicine, etc., and the professional or technical " management " staff in industry : the social position and psychology of these two classes are similar and, from some points of view, very important, but, for our present purposes, they can be ignored.) The socialist, whatever be his colour, starts by eliminating the first of these classes; he finds the ownership of economic resources and the control of industry con-centrated in the hands of the property-owners and capitalists, and he proposes to withdraw both and transfer them to the community. That means the elimination of the property-owner and capitalist as factors in the social life and the economic organization of the community. After this elimination the socialist is left in the following position. Industrially and economically society will now be divided into two great classes, the workers or producers of industrial commodities, and the consumers of those commodities. The ownership of economic resources and the control of production, now withdrawn from the capitalist classes, have to be vested in other hands.

Prima facie the socialist who has reached this theoretical position, and who has rejected State socialism, might take one of two alternative lines. He can make either production or consumption the basis of his socialistic organization of the community. If he choose the first alternative, he will make the producers the pivot upon which the whole life of society must turn : he will take the producers and their organizations and transfer to them the control over economic resources, over production and the instruments and methods of production; the community will be organized for production and the producer will take the place of the capitalist as the dominant force in society. On the other hand, he may look to the other great class, remaining after the elimination of the capitalist, to form the basis of social organization. For industrial purposes society will then be organized as a community of consumers, and the control of its resources and of production will be vested in organizations of consumers.

It must be said at once that the whole tendency of modern socialists and socialism is to adopt the first alternative. The Marxist, the syndicalist, the Guild Socialist, the Bolshevik, all, either consciously or unconsciously, regard the socialist commonwealth as a community of producers and look forward to a new world in which the control of the economic life of the community would be vested in the organized producers as representing the whole community. There can be no doubt that historical causes have very largely contributed to this tendency in socialism. Socialism is the science or religion of social revolt;

it was born in a revolt among the workers or producers
against the conditions which the tyranny and exploitation of capitalism inevitably imposed upon them. It
has become in the course of years an almost automatic
reaction of the capitalists' chief victims against the
" Hell of the wage-earner." Its most congenial and
fertile soil has been found in those organizations of
the worker-producers, the trade unions, whose main
function it is to carry on an incessant struggle against
the capitalist controllers of industry and to wring from
them by militant methods, the only methods recognized by the savagery of our civilization, some
additional share in the profits of industrial production
or some slight control over the conditions of their
employment. This environment of the militant producer, in which socialism has grown up, has naturally
had a deep effect upon its outlook. In the conflict
of the capitalist system what is taken from the worker
is added to the capitalist, and what is wrung from the
capitalist becomes the spoil of the producer. The Red
Flag of socialism becomes the banner under which the
producer fights this fight against capitalism, and, if
final and complete victory should go to Labour, the
capitalist would be eliminated and the proletariat of
producers would alone remain to control the socialist
commonwealth. Thus it is that the socialist commonwealth comes to be accepted as a community of
industrial producers, and the socialist looks forward
to a socialist society organized on the basis of production and in which the control of industry is vested
in producers' organizations, glorified trade unions,
Guilds, or soviets.

Recognition of the fact that the present function
of the producers' organization is rightly to fight for

its own hand against the capitalist and his system, and sympathy with the aspirations of the worker, ought not to lead us without further investigation to accept production as the basis and the producers' organization as the unit in socialistic society. The very fact that one of our beliefs or aspirations can be traced to a historical cause should make us view it with suspicion, for the probability is that it has been partly infected by some ancient illusion or some deep-seated and traditional evil in the individual or the communal mind. This is particularly true of the socialist beliefs with which I have been dealing. They spring, as we have seen, directly from the capitalist psychology which, while capitalism still exists, is imposed upon the worker in his struggle for existence against the capitalist. The socialist must, therefore, satisfy himself that, by carrying over into the new world of a socialist commonwealth beliefs and desires which had their roots in the psychology of capitalism, he will not be doing for socialism precisely what the 19th century democrat did for democracy by carrying over into the new world of reformed Parliaments, universal suffrage, etc., the psychology of oligarchy. The hardest part of the socialist's task, as the recent history of Russia shows, will perhaps be, not the elimination of the capitalist, but the elimination of the psychology of the capitalist from the society which has been constituted in accordance with all the formal principles of socialism. If the communal beliefs and desires now existing with regard to production and consumption persist, the community may have a socialistic body, but it will certainly have a capitalistic soul.

This raises the elementary question of the position

of production and consumption, of the producer and consumer, in a socialist society. As stated here, it may at first sight seem to be so elementary, academic, and theoretical that many people will regard with impatience the prospect of a whole chapter devoted to its consideration. But of all the beliefs which lie behind the actions of men in masses it is the most elementary and the most fundamental which are the least academic and theoretical. It is these beliefs which are the strongest bulwarks of ancient evils and the greatest bar to progress. Hidden, as a rule, beneath the surface of our consciousness, they form an invisible barrier against which new ideas or aspirations beat helplessly, and, if after a long time some new idea at last does succeed in penetrating through the barrier into the communal mind, it has long since lost all its freshness and virtue and is already assimilated to and undistinguishable from the old. I may say at once that, in my opinion, socialists have been wrong in accepting, often unconsciously, their view of production and the producer from existing society, that syndicalism, communism, and Guild Socialism might create a formally socialistic society, but their attitude towards and the place which they assign to industrial production would make the growth of a socialistic psychology impossible; and finally that socialism implies consumption as the basis of communal organization. It is because the Co-operative Movement bases the organization of industry upon consumption and provides an instrument through which the control of industry might be given to the community, organized as consumers, that I believe that it might be used as one of the most powerful means for attaining the ideals of socialism. But the

practical question of the organization of a fully
socialistic society, and of the method of transition
from the capitalist society of to-day to the socialistic
society of to-morrow, cannot be adequately treated
unless we are absolutely clear in our minds as to this
elementary question of the position which should be
given to production and to consumption in the organization of the community.   I propose, therefore, to
discuss this question in the next chapter : we shall
then be in a position to examine the part which the
co-operative principle should play in a fully developed
socialistic society, and the part which the existing
Co-operative Movement might play in the transition
to socialism.

CHAPTER III.

PRODUCTION AND CONSUMPTION.

Many people will think that this chapter is "academic," but it is nothing of the sort. The socialist aims at creating a completely new form of society, but he is not Jehovah, he cannot say " let there be socialism " with any hope that on the following sabbath a complete socialist commonwealth will be established in the present seats and citadels of capitalism. In every revolution, which is a radical change in human institutions, there must be a process of destruction accompanied or followed by a lengthy process of construction. It is in this transition stage of construction that revolutions have always failed, and they have failed not because men have been unable to devise means for accomplishing the ends desired, but because they have been in confusion or disagreement with regard to what ends were ultimately desirable. Man is so ingenious and cunning an animal that he has always found it easy to devise means for attaining the evils and miseries which he desires for himself and his fellow-men, and there is no reason to believe that he could not be just as successful in attaining good and happiness if he really desired and had a clear idea of them.

This is particularly true of socialism. The end aimed at by the socialist is a highly complicated one, a new and intricate form of society; unless he and those who carry through the revolution have a clear idea of what that form of society should be, they will

certainly go astray as soon as they are immersed in
the tangle of practical problems which constitutes the
period of transition and, like the democrats of the
19th century, they will wake up one morning to
find that they have laboriously created hell in mistake
for heaven.   If the world wants a form of society
different from that which has produced the ruin of
the war and the even greater ruin of the peace, it
must have a clear idea of the ultimate form of that
society which it desires, for without such an idea it
cannot with safety take a single step in the transition
stage towards its attainment.

The place which we propose to assign to industrial
production in the ultimate socialistic commonwealth
is not an academic one ; it is the first practical problem
which the socialist has to consider. If we are to solve
this problem it is essential that we should free our
minds, as far as possible, from those beliefs and
prejudices which we inherit with the psychology of
capitalism ; and I propose, therefore, to examine
briefly the beliefs and desires with regard to production
and consumption which are accepted by the ordinary
man to-day.

The most striking characteristic of our society is
the enormous importance assigned to production, and
particularly industrial production, and the immense
part which they play in the lives of individuals. The
great majority of the population spend the greater
part of their waking existence in producing industrial
commodities, and a very large portion of the
remainder spend theirs in selling these commodities to
other people. This is what constitutes the " work "
of millions of men and women, and we not only
believe that a man's work is the most important thing

in his life, but we so organize society that in fact it
is so. It is upon this system and psychology of
" work " or production that the hierarchy of classes
in the capitalist community is built. A man's class
is determined by the work which he performs or does
not perform, by his production or his non-production.
Nevertheless, society under capitalism is so organized
that both the framework and machinery and the
psychology of production are extraordinarily incoherent and irrational. The position of a class in the
hierarchy of classes is determined by the nature of
the commodity which the class produces. At first
sight it might appear that the position of a class is
in inverse proportion to the amount of its production,
for the highest position in society is given to those
classes which produce nothing. But this principle of
social organization is applied sparingly and at only
one end of the social scale. Capitalism encourages
the rentier, whether he be a land-owner, a lawyer,
an author, a capitalist, or a gentleman " of no
occupation," to produce nothing; but it is prepared to
use the whole power of the State and the effective
weapon of starvation to compel the miner or the
railwayman to work. Non-production, therefore,
which is a virtue in one class, may be a crime in
another.

The position and reward of classes is also partly
and erratically determined by the social value of the
commodity which the class produces. The social
position of the brain-worker is higher than that of
the manual worker, and the highest paid industrial
worker can never hope to obtain anything approaching
the position or income of a successful writer, barrister,
or employer. This system is defended on the ground

that what brain-work produces must always be of higher social value than what manual labour produces. But, even if the defence be admitted, it is clear that the principle is only partially and erratically applied. The social value of drainage in a large modern city is immense, while that of champagne is negligible; but it is not easy to detect any influence of this fact upon the relative positions and earnings of sewer-men and wine-merchants.

The most powerful factor in the organization of the hierarchy of classes upon the basis of production is, however, profit-making. The position and reward of a class is mainly determined by the power which it possesses to levy a toll upon society. Practically the whole of production in the world to-day is on a basis of profit-making. No one produces anything unless he thinks that he can sell it, and the difference in the position and in the reward of different individuals and classes depends to a very great extent upon whether or not they are in a strong position for selling the commodity which they produce or the service which they perform. The strength or weakness of their position as vendors or profit-makers is only to a negligible extent determined by the nature of what they have to sell or by its value to the purchasers or consumers; it depends mainly upon two factors : first, the amount of control which the individual or class can exercise over the machine and instruments of production, and, second, their power of establishing a monopoly and creating a shortage of supplies. Thus under the present system both the capitalist and labour are continually attempting to sell commodities and services to the community at the highest profit possible, and the worker is forced to conform to the

rules of the capitalist game, i.e., to attempt, through
trade union organization and the ultimate threat of
withdrawing labour, to exact a monopoly price for
that labour. In this curious game the worker, until
comparatively recent times, always lost; the position
from which he started in his attempt to levy a toll
upon the community was much weaker than that of
either the capitalist or the professional classes. The
capitalist started with a control of the machine of
production and the possession of material resources;
no capitalist has ever been literally starved into
submission either by labour or by the community;
the question for him is one not between starvation
and a profit, but between a larger or smaller profit.
The professional classes, again, until the war destroyed the foundations of civilization over large
areas in Europe, were in a very strong position for
exacting monopoly prices for their services; they had
established, behind the wire entanglements of the
law or of social customs and institutions, an elaborate
system for controlling the entrance to their professions
and the supply of services; when they sallied out to
raid the community they always knew that, even if
the raid proved a failure, they would have this
impregnable position to fall back upon; before the
war there is no instance in which skilled lawyers or
doctors were starved into economic submission by
their employers or by the community. But even
to-day the economic position from which the industrial
worker starts to raid the community and to exact
a monopoly price for his labour is extremely weak. He
has no property, and the price at which hitherto he
has been able to sell his labour has made it impossible
to create any substantial reserve; instead of the law

and social institutions protecting his position, he finds, as soon as there is any chance of his becoming strong, that the whole machinery of the law and the power of the State are used to prevent his withdrawing his labour and exacting a monopoly profit for it.*   The profit which the industrial worker has been able to exact from the economic struggle has, in fact, been low, because the capitalist and the community can use against him the effective weapon of starvation enforced by the law, the army, and the police.

All these conditions acting together have produced in modern man a very peculiar and, as I think, irrational psychology and philosophy of production. That psychology is now automatically accepted in part by all of us, but, unless it is eradicated, no really socialistic form of society is possible.   The fact that the majority of human beings only produce in order that they may earn a living, i.e., in order that they may not be starved to death, and that the criterion of production is not anything in the thing produced, but the amount of profit which the individual can make out of producing it, has had this effect, that we unconsciously regard production as an end in itself. A man's work, i.e., production, is the most important thing in his life, but it is important simply because it is production and also because it " earns him his living," not because of any quality in the commodity produced.   Qualities in champagne and drainage, for instance, their social utility or their æsthetic value, do not really enter at all into the mental attitude of the manufacturer of champagne, the wine-merchant, and the sewer-man towards their occupations, nor indeed into the mental attitude of the rest of the community towards them. The first thing of importance is that a man should " work," that he should produce something, whether champagne or sewers is not of any great moment; the second thing of importance—and what differentiates one occupation from another—is the amount of profit which the production of champagne or sewers brings to the producers.

According to this social psychology we believe at the back of our minds that production should be organized and carried on, partly in order that " things " may be produced which are capable of being sold, and partly that people may earn a living, make a profit, or have an occupation. There are, however, other beliefs and desires with regard to production and work which in some periods of the world's history have had quite an appreciable effect upon civilization and which still have some influence upon the psychology of production. Some people have accepted, and even practised, the idea that the value of production depends upon the value of the thing produced, and that a man who spends eight hours a day and six days a week the whole of a life long, producing bad, ugly, and useless things, even though he earn a living wage or a profit of 25 per cent., cannot be said to live a life worthy of a civilized human being. According to this view the value of production depends upon one of two things, or upon both, upon the social or æsthetic value of the product or upon the mental attitude of the producer towards his work. The meaning and implication of the first of these two conditions are clear : no man should produce anything unless it be either good in itself or a means to good, and society, in so far as it

organizes production, should take as the standard of
production not the quantity of things produced or
the profit accruing to individuals or classes or the
amount of work provided to fill up the lives of the
citizens, but the kind of things produced for consumption by the community and the standard or quality
of life which production enables the community to
live.   Though most people would accept these statements of principles as theoretically sound, the whole
of modern production is, as we have seen, organized
on principles diametrically opposed to it.   But this
has not always been the case in the world's history.
In ancient Greece the principle, as here stated, was
not only universally accepted as a theory, but to a
very large extent it was applied in the lives of the
individual and in the organization of the Greek State
and Greek society.   Ancient Athens was, indeed,
neither a heaven nor a Utopia, and human beings
there, not exempt from the ferocious stupidity which
appears to be characteristic of their species, inflicted
upon themselves and one another relatively almost
as much misery and cruelty as we ourselves succeed in
inflicting with the experience of another two thousand
years behind us.   Nevertheless, there is much to be
said for the view that communal life has never before
or since reached the high level of civilization and
humanity which it did in Athens during the fourth
century before Christ.   If this be correct the real
cause of this curious phenomenon of a civilized human
society will be found, I think, in the fact that the
Greeks had a curious theory of production and that
they actually applied it in the everyday life of their
society.   Even the jokes in their comic operas show
that they conceived the objects of their existence as

something really different from what we conceive ours
to be. They set an immense value upon beauty,
intellectual activity, leisure, and happiness; they had
no idea that the right life for a man to live is one
of incessant work in order that he or someone else
may make a profit or even that he or someone else
may receive a spiritual reward in heaven after death.
The " good life," which in their opinion was the end
to be aimed at both by the individual and the community, was a life of great freedom and activity; but
their activities were not economic, they were æsthetic,
intellectual, political, and simply physical.   Thus
athletics and physical enjoyment in sport and games
formed part of the " good life " in a well-ordered
State; and the organized life of society was directed
mainly to the production of beautiful cities, the public
performance of dramatic works of art, to the provision
of political oratorical displays and causes célèbres,
and to war. It is true that full citizenship was
restricted to a very small class in the community and
that at the other end of the scale slavery existed, but
22 centuries ago in Athens the gulf between the free
citizen and the slave was far less than it is to-day in
London between the free rentier with an income of
many thousands a year and the free sweated worker.
The mass of the population consisted of " small
farmers or craftsmen," and there was no economic
exploitation of slaves on a large scale, as in later times
there was in Rome. At no time in the history of
the world has there existed a highly developed civilization in which there was such an equal distribution
of wealth as there was in Athens, and this followed
directly from the fact that both in theory and in
practice the object of production to the Greek was

not production or profit, but use. In fact, we might
now be living in a civilized Europe if the Greeks had
not believed that war is one of the chief objects of
organized society, and if they had realized that war
is incompatible with the " good life."

The Greek view of production has never, perhaps,
completely perished, and until the 19th century a
vague idea persisted in Europe that the main object
of production was to produce things either beautiful
or useful. But, partly owing to a characteristic of
human nature and partly owing to the spread of
certain doctrines of Christianity, a new conception
with regard to production grew up and still has considerable influence upon society. Under certain
circumstances there is undoubtedly much pleasure to
be obtained from the mere act of production ; the
artist or the skilled craftsman notoriously finds a keen
" joy in his work." The idea that this " joy in one's
work " is one of the objects of production has often
been and still is widely held, and it has become confused with another idea largely due to Christianity.
Christianity taught the useful and dangerous doctrine
that God had ordered the universe in such a way
that each individual was born in a certain station of
life in which it was his duty contentedly to perform
his allotted function. Hence it is deduced that
Providence has ordained that the miner shall mine,
the champagne-merchant sell champagne, the sewer-
man keep the sewers in order, and the capitalist make
a profit, and by a not unnatural extension of this
theory it is further deduced that each of these
individuals should find in his occupation " the joy
in work."

The relation between these various and conflicting

elements in the psychology of production, and the actual development and organization of modern industrial production, are most important. Capitalist industry does not, as we have seen, produce things because they are beautiful, good, or useful, but because someone thinks that he will be able to induce other people to buy them and that thereby he will make a profit for himself. For all the classes engaged in production, other than the manual worker, this motive of profit-making has hitherto proved adequate; the reward which may conceivably fall to the successful capitalist, financier, employer, manager, professional expert, is so great that on what may be called the capitalist side there has been an ever-growing competition to produce commodities. But the " joy in work " or in creation or production scarcely enters at all into the psychology of these " producers," and the only quality of the product which is of real importance to them is its saleability, its marketableness. The man, other than the manual worker, who starts to produce matches or books does not do so because he believes matches or books to be good things, or even that people want matches or books, but simply because he believes that he can induce people to buy those commodities at a price higher than it costs him to produce them. That is why during the last hundred years of capitalism more and more energy has been put into the work, not of producing things, but of inducing people to believe that they want to buy things which are produced. The psychology of production among persons other than the manual workers consists almost entirely of two principles : produce what is saleable and sell at a profit.

But the position of the industrial manual worker is different, and the development of his psychology has therefore been different. The commodity which he has been engaged in selling is industrial manual labour, and his weak economic position, as we saw in the last chapter, results in his making very little profit out of the transaction. His work is arduous and usually unpleasant, and his reward is small. The consequence is that from the very first there has been a tendency for the capitalist industrial system to break down owing to the producer's refusal to produce.

The manual worker finds himself in the centre of a system which assumes that you will only produce if you make a profit out of production; he then discovers that if he increases his effort to produce all or the greater part of the profit goes into the pocket of someone else. Hence the almost universal phenomenon among workers of ca' canny, a phenomenon which is not a proof of original sin in the worker, but of the fact that the very conditions of capitalist industry have resulted in making the main motive for capitalist production inoperative in the case of the majority of the producers. The great mass of manual workers are forced to produce, because if they did not they would starve; their object is to sell the minimum amount of their labour at the maximum price, and they will not increase that minimum, and therefore production, because the profit from the increase would go not to them, but to someone else. That is the logic and the psychology of our system of production.

As the industrial system of the 19th century developed it became more and more doubtful whether fear of starvation was an adequate motive, whether it

could obtain from the worker the volume of production and the regular flow of products necessary for
the continuance of our urban civilization. The war
has considerably increased the doubt, because it has
made the worker more conscious of his own dissatis-
faction and because people no longer believe that
death, by starvation or otherwise, is so important or
terrible a thing as it seemed to their fathers. The
existing organization of society requires that large
numbers of people will have a sufficient motive for
continuing to produce by working eight hours or more
per day for a pre-war wage of between £1 and £2 per
week, and there is evidence that the whole system is
breaking down, because the motive no longer works.
In many parts of Europe there are already considerable numbers of industrial workers who seem prepared
to starve themselves and other people rather than to
continue to produce on the old conditions.

This tendency of the capitalist system of production
to breakdown on the refusal of the worker to produce
has always existed; in order to counteract it, conscious
and unconscious attempts have been made, not without success, to enlist those other beliefs about and
motives for production which we have just examined.
The result is the confused and irrational psychology
of production which exists to-day even among industrial workers. In the early part of the 19th century
the Christian doctrine of production was still widely
accepted in its undiluted form, and the vast mass of
the population believed that for the miner to refuse
to mine or the spinner to spin would be a sin against
the laws both of God and of England. Most of the
" upper classes," even when they have ceased to
believe in God or Christianity, continue to hold this

view in a slightly modified form, namely, that it is a moral duty or a duty to the community that the worker should continue to work. But it would be a great mistake to imagine that the view is confined to the capitalist or " upper " classes; it permeates the workers themselves. This will be apparent to anyone who, when a big strike of, say, miners or railwaymen threatens the community, will take the trouble to discuss it with wage-earners who are not personally interested in it. He will find that quite a number of these wage-earners are morally indignant not that miners or engine drivers should demand higher wages, but that they should refuse even for a fortnight to drive engines or hew coal. These beliefs are often neither conscious nor articulate, but it is clear that these people still do believe that it is a moral duty to " work " and to go on " working " in the sphere to which Providence has assigned you.

I do not believe that, unless this curious superstition had been widely and deeply spread among industrial workers, our system of production could possibly have persisted as long as it has. But it is even more remarkable that our tottering capitalist system has also been bolstered up by the doctrine that the industrial worker can and should find in his occupation " the joy in work." The fact is remarkable because the whole tendency of industrial development has been to eliminate every particle and possibility of human interest or enjoyment from the operations of the human agents in production. It is often argued that it is possible to exaggerate this tendency, that much of modern industry demands a high degree of skill in the worker, and that wherever work demands skill the worker can find the artist's or the craftsman's

" joy in production." And these optimists often add
that human beings fortunately are not all built on
the same pattern, and that, if the development of
machinery makes it inevitable that a large part of
production consists in the unintelligent repetition of
mechanical movements, some people—in fact, the
majority of the industrial workers—are so constituted
that they find " joy " in the unintelligent repetition
of a mechanical movement.

We are here getting very near the core of this
problem of production and society, for we are face to
face with a crucial question which very few people,
even among socialists and democrats, will face. At
the time of the last Census, out of 13 million males
above the age of ten, 9 millions were recorded as
being engaged in commerce and industry, and it is
no exaggeration, therefore, to say that two-thirds of
the adult male population spend the whole of their
life in ceaseless mechanical or laborious operations
which a Greek, who lived 2,000 years before we
discovered the secret of civilization, would have
considered unworthy of a human being. I believe
that, if our minds were not warped by the distorted
psychology of capitalist production, we should agree
with the Greek. If civilization as we know it is to
continue, it may be necessary that two-thirds of the
population spend eight hours a day in either hewing
coal, or adding up columns of figures, or punching
tram tickets, or lifting heavy weights, or putting a
label on to a bottle of champagne, or putting a minute
portion of a useless and ugly article into a machine—
it may be necessary, but it is hypocrisy to pretend
that our civilization is civilized or that our society
can ever be anything but an aristocracy or oligarchy

based upon industrial slavery. There were writers, thinkers, and reformers in the 19th century who saw and admitted these facts, and they proposed as a solution to return, by one method or another, to the pre-industrial form of society. They were usually people who believed that the justification for production lay in the producer's " joy in his work," and they proposed to bring back this " joy in work " through the breaking up of large scale capitalist industry, through producers' co-operation and the self-governing workshop, or through the return to a system of arts and crafts. But the disease of a bad and false psychology of production has eaten far too deeply into our society for it to be touched by these well-meaning, homœopathic sentimentalists. You have only to walk in a city like London or Manchester to see that this psychology and machinery, and the intricate organization of men and machines which we call industry, have got such a grip over us that only either a violent upheaval, a complete breakdown, or a fundamental change in our psychology and social organization can liberate us. In Eastern Europe the liberation has already been effected partly by upheaval and partly by breakdown, and the whole system of organized industrial production has collapsed because upon its rotten foundations there accumulated at last a load of intolerable injustice. Short-sighted people comfort themselves with the belief that it is war or revolution which has produced this collapse and has converted three-quarters of Europe to the verge of starvation, and that war is due to the wickedness of the German and revolution to the wickedness of the Russian. But war and revolution are only the symptoms of social disease or the by-products of our social beliefs and of our industrial organization. The whole of Europe is now threatened with the fate which, in various degrees, has already overtaken every belligerent country east of the Rhine. But the important thing to observe is that the collapse of the industrial system of capitalism does not mean the end of industrialism. Even in Russia, Poland, and Austria there is no return to the age of Guilds or arts and crafts. The towns decay, but industrialism which we associate with the machine and the factory remain. In Russia the Communists have already begun to build, upon the ruins of the old system, a new elaborate machinery of industrialized production; elsewhere, though the factories may stand idle and the factory worker starve or die of typhus, there is no sign of production being organized otherwise than on the factory system.

It is practically certain that the large-scale production of the factory system, with its minute subdivision of labour and its complicated organization, will continue. Europe may quite possibly sink back into the poverty and barbarism of the Middle Ages, but our new barbarism will remain combined with the industrial barbarism of the 19th century. It is in this situation that the socialist comes forward with an alternative to the already half-derelict capitalist system. In putting forward his alternative he has to allow both for the permanence of industrialism and the existing psychology of production which we have examined in the preceding pages.

Modern socialism, while rightly proceeding on the assumption that industrialism must continue, seems to me to have committed the fatal error of accepting a large part of the existing psychology of production.

make my position quite clear, sum up what I conceive
to be the psychology of production accepted by the
industrial worker upon whom and upon whose beliefs
and desires the socialist must build. The industrial
worker may be said to have reached a stage at which
he is definitely opposed to the capitalist system. He
is ready to accept the socialization of industry. He
would gladly eliminate the capitalist and the competitive, profit-making, or " profiteering " elements
in the industrial organization. But his whole attitude
towards industry and production is still necessarily
capitalistic. He regards an occupation or vocation
primarily from the point of view of what kind of a
living can be made out of it, and his standard of
desirability is a minimum of work for a maximum of
pay. That is not a socialist but a capitalist standard.
I am not blaming anyone in saying this, I am stating
a fact, and a fact that the socialist will ignore at
his peril. It is inevitable that the worker, fighting
with his back against the wall in the very centre of
the economic civil war, which we call modern civilization, should adapt himself to his environment; if
he did not, he would economically perish. To the
industrial producer production, therefore, is primarily
a means to providing himself with an occupation or
work and a " living," and he aims at a maximum
monetary return for a minimum of work. Further—
and this is a most important point—the trade union,
which is the organ of the organized producers, is a
weapon of economic war, and the worker rightly
to-day regards the object of his organizations to be
the protection of his own interests in the struggle
against the other classes in the community or even

of one section of the workers against another section.
The revolt of the worker is not against the fact that
he has to devote practically the whole of his life to
industrial production and that his work is long,
laborious, and mechanical, while the thing produced
may be and frequently is shoddy, ugly, and useless;
his revolt is mainly against the fact that he makes
so little out of his work or so much less than other
classes make out of their work.

The industrial worker also unconsciously accepts
the doctrine which capitalistic Christianity has
instilled into him, that he should regard his " work,"
irrespective of what his work produces, as the
supremely important thing in his life, that one's
trade or profession, provided that one exercises it
conscientiously, is something good in itself, something
to be proud of, and that a man can be civilized whose
main activity from youth to the grave consists in,
say, pulling a lever, or adding up columns of figures,
or converting truth into journalistic lies.

By saying this I do not wish to imply that it is
a bad thing for a man to take a pride in work or in
production.   Probably nothing really good can be
produced unless the producer experiences the " joy
in production " and takes a pride in his work. What
I do say is that we shall not begin to be civilized
until, both individually and socially, we realize that
the value of production and work depends upon the
value of the product and the quality of the productive
activity. A man who with speed and skill performs
some simple, mechanical action necessary for the
production of some shoddy article by a machine is
better than a man who performs the same action
badly; if you have to add up columns of figures, it

is better to add them correctly than incorrectly; and if you do spend your time writing articles for the Press, which are lies and which you know to be lies, it is possibly better to write them skilfully than to write them unskilfully. But that does not alter the fact that none of these occupations are such that they ought to furnish the main activity of any man's life, and any society which acquiesces in the fact that three-quarters of the population find their main activities in such occupations remains in the stage of barbarism.

The truth is that industrial production is now a necessary evil, and it should be recognized as such both by society and by producers. We should aim at reducing it to a minimum consistent with a " good life " and a certain standard of material comfort in the community. It should not form the principal occupation of any class or any individual in the community, but should be recognized as a necessary communal evil to be borne equally by every member of the community. The attitude of society towards industrial production should, in fact, be that of the individual towards certain daily actions which he performs for his own personal convenience. Most people are compelled by climate and convention to spend a certain amount of their time each day putting on and taking off a considerable number of articles of clothing; many men perform a somewhat elaborate process for removing the hair from their face, and many women perform an even more elaborate process, by means of pins and other contrivances, for making more conspicuous the hair on the top of their heads. Most sensible people, however, aim at reducing the time spent on these operations to a minimum. A man

who spent the whole of his day in putting on and
taking off his trousers, or a woman who spent the
whole of hers in putting on and taking off her stays,
would be placed by us in an asylum, and yet we view
with equanimity and even approval a social organization which compels millions of men and women to
spend their whole day in putting on or taking off the
trousers and stays of the community.

Socialists and many industrial workers look forward
to and desire a social revolution, but, though they
may change the outer crust of society, they will never
change the essential character of it, unless they effect
a revolution in their attitude and that of other people
towards production and consumption.   The false
psychology and philosophy of production, which I
have analysed in the preceding pages, result in a
failure to distinguish between the relative value of
different products and productive activities, as well
as between the relative social value of production and
consumption.   Both the standard of civilization in
a community and the value of an individual depend
partly on their consumption, partly on their production, and partly on their productive activity.   For
instance, industry should be considered by the
community not from the point of view of production,
but solely from that of consumption.   It is in the
nature of modern machine industry that it does not
produce things which are good in themselves; its
only justification is that it is capable of turning out
a large number of similar material products with little
expenditure of human effort.   Those products may
be useful, but, being products of large-scale production, they must almost always lack those qualities
which are necessary for the production of something

good in itself, like a work of art. The actual activity
which this modern industry requires from the
industrial worker is for the most part mechanical and
unpleasant, and the more efficient industry becomes
the less skill and initiative it demands from the human
agent in production. Hence not only has the industrial
product normally no value in itself, but the
industrial activity of the human agent has normally
a negative value. But this means that the sole
function of industry should be to produce things which
are useful, i.e., those things which it is necessary for
the community and individual to consume in order
that they may exercise those other activities which
constitute civilization in a society or the " good life "
in an individual.

The society and the individual alike require certain
material things and certain services, such as food,
transport, boots, sanitation, which are good only in
the sense that they are useful, in the sense that they
make it possible for the society or the individual to
pursue other activities, whether of production or
consumption, which are good in themselves. That is
the secret of the " good life " of which those
barbarians in Athens two thousand years ago had a
glimmer, but which our generation has almost completely lost. We have lost the secret of living well,
primarily because Christianity and capitalism between
them have given us a false standard of values both
in consumption and production and in commodities.
Large-scale industry is peculiarly fitted for the production of those " useful " commodities which have
no value in themselves, but which must be produced
if human beings are to have the opportunity of living
both happily and well. It can turn out commodities,

like food, clothing, furniture, with immense rapidity
and efficiency at infinitely less cost in human exertion
than either the human producer unaided by the
machine or even small-scale machine production.
Industrialism, guided by a little reason or imagination,
might have revolutionized the life of man, might have
raised him in a generation as high above his civilization in the pre-industrial age as the civilization of
the 18th century, through a process of tedious
evolution, stood above the civilization of the
chimpanzee.   But industrialism, which might have
almost freed man completely from the curse of Adam,
which is to spend the whole of his life and his days
eating bread in the sweat of his face, has actually
increased the sum and burden of grinding and
deadening labour.   If without sentimentality or
prejudice we were to estimate in terms of human
happiness and social progress the chief results of all
the industrial inventions of the 18th and 19th
centuries, we should be compelled to say that they
are summed up in the difference between the slums
of Manchester and the slums of Constantinople and
in the difference between the battlefields of the Somme
or Flanders and the battlefield of Waterloo.

The causes of this curious phenomenon are to be
found, as the socialist holds, in capitalism, or rather,
as I think, in Christianity and capitalism and in the
psychology of production which is at once both the
cause and effect of a Christianized capitalist society.
That psychology views industrial productions from the
angle of production, profit, and work.   It makes no
distinction between productive activities which are
good in themselves and those which are either neutral
or positively bad, as may be seen by considering for

a moment the attitude of Church, State, and society
towards the activities of respectively the miner, stock-
broker, artist, scientist, teacher, and brewer. It
makes little or no distinction between products, for
it judges production quantitatively or by the standard
of individual profit. Civilization consists for it not
in the quality of products and consumption, but in
the volume and variety of commodities produced.

Socialism should, I suggest, build on not only a
totally different organization, but also a totally
different psychology of production and consumption.
Its standard of civilization would be the level of
quality in the consumption and activities of the
community. But that would entail an even more
important revolution than most professional revolu-
tionaries contemplate. It would require to a very
great extent a shifting in the angle of vision of both
society and the individual from production to consumption. For the socialist would always begin by
asking what is the quality of a community's activities
and of the products which it consumes? From this
point of view the individual's work has little or no
importance either to him or to the community. That
he should produce is not important, but what he
produces may be of importance, because it is
consumed. The ultimate aim of the socialist would
therefore be a society in which the activities of
individuals were good in themselves and the products
were good in themselves. But that would immediately
put industry and industrial production into a position
which they certainly do not occupy in the society
of to-day or in that which most socialists appear to
contemplate. For neither the products of industry
nor the activities of the industrial producers are good

in themselves. Industry should be confined to the
production of commodities which it is necessary for
society and the individual to consume in order that
it and he may do or produce other things. We must
make a rigid distinction between industrial production
and the activities involved in industrial production on
the one hand and non-industrial production and
activities on the other. We should no longer attempt
to produce industrially things which are, for instance,
beautiful, but only things which are useful, which
are, in the simplest sense, necessaries of life.
Industrial production would thus be regarded solely
from the angle of consumption, communal consumption, a minimum consumption compatible with the
comfort and real activities of the community. The
domination of society by the machine and the factory
would no longer be tolerated, and it would be regarded
as intolerable that any man should fill his life with
" work." Once that psychology of production and
consumption were grasped, we should rapidly see that
it is infinitely more important for a society or
individual that a man or woman should enjoy or
produce a play or a book or a picture, or should play
football or dance, or should talk or go on the river
or picnic or cultivate a garden or teach children and
adults or make love to one another than that they
should make the fraction of some article which is
neither beautiful nor useful.

If the conclusion at which we have now arrived
be the true one, then the socialist must aim at getting
these beliefs and desires with regard to consumption
and production accepted by men and women, and at
so moulding the framework of society that it will
encourage the growth of this new psychology of

production and at the same time gradually receive
the imprint of and be filled and vitalized by its spirit.
The Co-operative Movement seems to me important
simply because it has developed a system of industry
containing the germs of such a psychology and
organization. Co-operators are the only controllers
of industry, capable of large-scale production, who
have begun to look at industrial production from this
angle of use or consumption. They form but a small
island in the great sea of capitalist industry, they have
to take part in the perpetual competitive struggle
which capitalism imposes upon them, they, like all
of us, unconsciously accept the psychology of their
capitalist environment; their grasp of their own
principle is therefore often vague and vacillating, and
it is easy enough to find stones to cast at them and
their Movement; but for nearly eighty years now
the Movement has been growing steadily in all
directions and developing an organization which
reflects and is inspired by this principle that industrial
production should be carried on not for the purpose
of providing anyone with profit or with work, but
solely in order to provide the material commodities
necessary for use or consumption by the community.

The socialist has a two-fold task. He is looking
forward to what people call a utopia. He believes
that it would be possible even out of the irrational,
semi-barbarous, and elusive material of human
nature as it exists to-day to produce a society in which
three-quarters of the evil and misery which we inflict
upon ourselves and one another would be abolished.
Here he is concerned to see, by peering into the future,
the broad outline of the form or organization and
also the spirit of such a community. That task is

neither academic nor utopian. It is so easy and so disastrous in politics to be practical, to refuse to consider what is ultimately desirable and possible. Looking round the world to-day one sees little but communal misery and savagery : a class struggle in which all the most savage and sordid of human passions, hatred, tyranny, exploitation, and cupidity, are encouraged until every now and then they break out into White or Red terrors and massacres; and where men are not massacring one another in the name of economics, they are doing so in the name of nationalism or freedom, Englishmen massacring Irishmen, Mesopotamian Arabs, Egyptians, and Indians in order to convince them that freedom and happiness are only to be obtained within the British Empire, and Irishmen, Mesopotamian Arabs, Egyptians and Indians massacring Englishmen in order to prove the contrary. I do not believe that people would tolerate this barbarism if they had even an imperfect vision of what they might make of the world or of that corner of the world in which they live. In the past whenever there has been some rare progress towards a civilization it has always accompanied a vision, however imperfect, of what the practical man would call an earthly utopia and a belief in the attainability of that vision which has influenced political thought and moulded political action. A relapse into barbarism has, on the other hand, always been accompanied by a loss of political and social beliefs and ideals, a cynical opportunism which permeates society and ends in its anarchical dissolution. This is hardly astonishing, for neither an individual nor a community of individuals who have no conception of the direction in which they desire to go can expect to reach anything but disaster.

The socialist must, therefore, have some clear and broad vision of that ultimate socialist community which he considers possible and desirable. In the next chapter, therefore, I shall attempt to trace, in the light of those facts and principles which have emerged from the analysis of this chapter, the form of such a fully-developed socialist society and the part which the co-operative principle of industrial production might play in it.   But, having determined in broad outline the kind of society which we may aim at as ultimately realizable, the socialist has then to relate this ideal to the actual life of to-day which surrounds him. He has to consider how the transition may be made from the one to the other, how we might encourage the growth and development of those elements in our social psychology or organization which are in harmony with the ideal, and how we might destroy those elements which are in conflict with it. In the last chapter, therefore, I propose to deal with this transition period and the part which the Co-operative Movement might play in it.

CHAPTER IV.

THE CO-OPERATIVE COMMONWEALTH.

In this chapter we shall be discussing the kind of society which the socialist should aim at ultimately bringing into existence. It is not a utopia in the sense that we can let our imagination run riot to build up in the clouds the best of all possible worlds. This socialist commonwealth must be built upon earth and upon the earthy human beings whom we know. It is an ideal not indeed immediately attainable, but yet not obviously unattainable. It is, in fact, a society in which the principles and ideals of socialism, which we have been examining in the previous pages, would be operating fully and freely. What I now want to consider is the part which the co-operative system of industry might play in this possible, but not immediately attainable, world. Let us first examine the outlines of this socialist commonwealth as they have been drawn for us by the analysis, arguments, and conclusions of the previous chapters.

In our socialist commonwealth the basis of organization and the motive power in communal action must be common interests, and this not as an abstract and vaguely diffused ideal, but in every part of society and the machinery of society. To-day everyone finds himself born into a kind of framework of social machinery and organization which immediately impresses upon his mind the psychology of competition; the infant born into our socialist society must find himself in a framework of organization and machinery which impresses upon his mind the psychology of co-operation. The framework must therefore assume, as a foundation of society and of its organization, not a conflict of competing interests between class and class and individual and individual, but co-operation and common interests. Hence the ownership and control of the economic resources of the community, and the production and distribution of those commodities and services which form the material foundation of a reasonably comfortable life, must be vested not in private hands, but in the community.

Next, the socialist commonwealth will proceed to isolate, as far as possible, the production of the necessaries of a comfortable existence, which I shall call the necessaries of life, from the other activities of the community. It will act on the assumption that the object of industry is to produce those necessaries of life, food, clothing, transport, etc., which the community requires for its use. Industrial production would be controlled by the community for the community, and would be confined, with certain exceptions, to the production of these necessaries of life. The social organization and machinery of industry would reflect the belief that the object of industry is not to provide any man with work or an occupation, that the activities involved in industrial production are necessary but unpleasant and should, therefore, form the main occupation of no man's or woman's life, that everyone should perform his share of this unpleasant but necessary work, remaining free to find his main activities in other pursuits or occupations, and that industrial production should be rigidly confined to a minimum compatible with comfortable existence.

And now, reducing these general statements to a

more concrete form, I would conceive a society of
this kind working somewhat in the following way.
The land, mines, factories, ships, railways, and all
such financial machinery as was required would be
in communal ownership and under communal control.
Production and distribution would be controlled
democratically on a basis of use or consumption, that
is to say, the organized consumers would elect local
and national executives for this purpose. These
executives would estimate the minimum of necessaries
required by the community for comfortable material
existence and would organize industry solely with the
object of producing that minimum. The whole object
of this organization would be the production of the
greatest possible amount of the simplest material
commodities at the least expenditure of human effort.
Every member of the community would contribute
an equal amount of labour to the production of these
commodities and would receive in return a right to an
equal share in their use or consumption.

This is a very bare outline of the socialist commonwealth, and I must ask the reader to suspend judg-
ment upon it until this chapter is finished, until I
have filled in the details and considered the implica-
tions in and objections to the design. But before
doing this, I wish immediately to relate what I have
said to the principles and ideals of consumers' co-
operation. I maintain that the germs of such a society
are already contained in the Co-operative Movement
of to-day, that it already looks at and organizes
industry from this angle of use or consumption. It
begins by organizing the consumer locally and
nationally on a democratic basis, throwing the local
unit, the society, open to every member of the

community. The machinery of organization makes it
possible for the democracy of consumers, if they desire
it, to control through their units, the local societies
and the federations of local societies, the whole of
co-operative industrial production and distribution.
The present Movement is a very imperfect instrument;
co-operators have only a dim understanding of their
own principles or those of democracy; they are permeated, for the reasons given in the previous chapters,
by the unconscious psychology of capitalism; but
they have got hold somehow or other of this embryonic
idea or ideal of " production for use," and, in the
blind and fumbling way in which masses of men think
and act, are trying to translate it into the facts of
the world which surrounds them.   Only in the Co-
operative Movement does the organization of industry
allow the demand of the consumers directly to set in
motion and control production.   If one regards the
Movement   to-day   as   a   community   of   organized
consumers, one can observe a system actually at work
in which the processes of production or distribution,
whether in the Wholesale Society's factories or offices
or in the local stores, are set in motion and kept in
motion not by a desire to sell or a calculation of
possible profit, not by any desire or necessity to find
or provide " work," but by the knowledge of an
Executive,   elected   by   the   community,   that   the
community requires certain commodities and services
for its consumption or use.   A single example must
serve to show how in this way co-operation differs
and would differ from other systems of industrial
organization.   A capitalist or a company which started
to open a factory for the production of boots in
Leicester would only do so after a calculation of the

costs of production and the price at which the product
could be sold, and what would finally determine
whether the process of production should or should
not begin would be a calculation as to whether it would
or would not be possible to induce the community to
buy a certain quantity of the product at a price giving
a certain profit to the capitalist or company.   No
small proportion of the price and of the labour
involved in getting the product into the hands of the
consumers would consist of the cost and labour in
inducing the community to believe that it wanted to
pay that price for that particular capitalist's boots.
Again, under Guild Socialism or any other system
controlled by the producer, it is difficult to see how
the production of boots could be started or continued
in Leicester except under the impulse of the producers,
a demand of the producer, in fact, based upon what
is now sometimes called " the right to work."   But
the C.W.S. directors, when they decided to build and
run a boot factory, were concerned neither with profit
nor with " work "; they did not think of these things,
they thought only of the ascertained demand among
the members of Co-operative societies, the community
of consumers who had elected them, for boots.   It
was this requirement of the consumers for boots which
acted directly upon the organization of industry,
assembled the instruments of production at Leicester,
and now causes the boots to be produced.

The co-operative is the only system of industry
which establishes this direct and intimate relation
between consumption and production.   It does so
because its principle or ideal is democratic control by
the consumer and production for use, and also because
it has created the machinery capable of bringing the

consumer's demand to bear directly on the organization of production and of eliminating other motives for production. If the whole industry of this country were in the hands of the Co-operative Movement, and if the Movement embraced the whole population of the country, the Executives and Managements which were elected to control production and distribution would not try to induce people to take cheap watches and jewellery or most of the thousand and one commodities now advertized, nor would they endeavour to produce for the sake of production or of providing employment; they would produce and distribute through the stores only those things which their constituencies informed them that they required. That demand would be conveyed directly through the channels of the co-operative organization, the store, the local quarterly meeting, and the local committee, right up through the federation of societies to the national organization of the Co-operative Wholesale Society.

If the co-operative system were extended to embrace the whole population and the whole of industry, we should have the framework of a socialist society answering to those requirements which have emerged from the discussion in the previous chapters. We now have to examine rather more minutely the working of the machinery within such a framework, the possibility of its developing a socialist rather than a capitalist psychology in the community, and certain objections to the whole idea and conception which have probably already occurred to the reader. One point I may dispose of at once. I do not consider that I can legitimately be called upon to work out in minute detail the system which I advocate and show

that it will work in every one of these details. I am
not building a utopia which I say must be accepted
as workable and desirable both in the whole and in
its parts. I am proceeding rather by the methods of
the scientist who establishes the general conditions
necessary if a certain result is to be produced. By
analyzing the causes which produce existing conditions
in society, I claim to be able to say : "If you wish
to create a civilized social organization and psychology
you must at least establish the following general
conditions. There is nothing inherently impossible
in these conditions; they do not postulate a complete
revolution in the mind and manners of men. The
thing would work provided that this and that were
in existence. It is true that 'this' and 'that'
could not be established to-day nor yet, perhaps,
to-morrow; but they are not impossibles, they are
within sight, if not within reach ; they and the society
which they would bring into existence are visible goals
which should guide our footsteps as political animals."

The framework of society which we are to aim at
as ultimately desirable is not complicated. Its
essential features are these : the whole community
would be organized locally and nationally in organizations similar to those of the Co-operative Movement
to-day; the community, thus organized, would own
all land required for agricultural purposes, all
factories, and the instruments of production; it would,
therefore, retain in its own hands a monopoly of
industrial production; every member of the community would be required to contribute an equal share
towards the work of industrial production and would
receive the right to an equal share of the products
and services.

The first point to be noted is one which has already been partly dealt with. The co-operative commonwealth will be concerned only with industry and the production and distribution of industrial products and services. Everything, in my opinion, turns upon society realizing and making provision for the distinction between industrial activities and products and other activities and products. Three-quarters of the social and economic evils in existing society are due, as I have shown, to a false view and valuation of industrial production and products. But the same confusion reappears in the writings of nearly all socialists. Guild socialists, for instance, with whom, as the next chapter will show, I am up to a point in agreement, vitiate their ultimate aims by accepting this confusion from the existing psychology of production. Mr. Cole nowhere seems to realize the enormous difference in values between different activities and different products, and he therefore contemplates with equanimity the growth of a society which treats the teacher, the professional man, the scientist, the miner, and the writer all exactly the same. Give them, says Mr. Cole, control through the Guild over the conditions of their productive activities, and all will be well. This assumes that a man ought to be able to find satisfaction in devoting his life to coal mining or adding up figures or writing articles or performing one or two mechanical movements in conjunction with a machine. I deny this absolutely, and I deny that the activities involved in such work are comparable in value or in interest or pleasurableness with those of teaching, of medicine and surgery, of art and literature, of acting, of cultivating one's garden, or of playing cricket. I deny that any society would have the right to call itself civilized in which large masses of the population contentedly found their " avocations " in such industrial activities, which made no distinction between products, and which, therefore, organized itself on a basis of production. It may be that we have so tangled ourselves up in the irrational organization and psychology of industrialism that we shall never succeed in breaking free from the tyranny of machines and of our own beliefs and desires, and that, therefore, the best that we can hope for is a society in which the majority of people find their main occupation in the drudgery which we call work and in the organization of a Guild for the democratic control of this drudgery. I do not believe that this is the case, but, if it be, let us cease to pretend that the ideals of socialism are attainable or that man is capable of creating a civilized society.

In the socialist co-operative commonwealth industrial production would be a monopoly of the community organized as consumers in local units, which would be developments of the existing co-operative store or society, and in a national body, which would be a development of the Wholesale Society. Industry would primarily be confined to the production of houses and furniture, clothing, food, articles of obvious utility, and transport. The main object of such a society should be to reduce industrial production to a minimum, and yet by efficient organization to produce a high standard of material comfort. Many people, I am aware, will say at once that the whole idea is impossibly utopian. I cannot, of course, prove that it is workable; all I can do is to show what conditions would be necessary if it is to work, and why those conditions are not necessarily unattainable.

The real difficulty in a socialist society, and indeed
in every society, is to establish a rational correlation
between production and consumption, between
demand and supply. The difficulty is enormously
increased where, as has happened in our world, society
and its whole organization have encouraged an irrational correlation and a false and vicious standard of
values in consumption. Where a man produces what
he consumes there tends to be what I call a rational
correlation between production and consumption and
a true standard of values applied to material products.
A Robinson Crusoe, having himself to supply the
physical labour necessary for the production of what
are now industrial products, will consider primarily
their relative utility; he will aim at so using his labour
as to produce the greatest possible quantity of the
simplest and most useful commodities. The nearer
production is kept to consumption, i.e., in the more
primitive forms of society, the more likely it is that
this correlation and standard will obtain; and the
more complicated the organization of society becomes,
the more danger there is that they will cease to be
operative. Capitalism, as we saw, has deliberately
encouraged a different correlation and standard based
upon profit. Utilizing the separation between consumption and production, between the consumer and
producer, which results from the division of labour,
it has developed a most elaborate and efficient system
for stimulating a demand for commodities which can
be sold at a profit. Capitalism has so debauched and
debased our taste for material commodities that one
of the hardest tasks before the socialist will be to
establish a correlation between consumption and
industrial production based upon simplicity and utility.

I believe the early co-operators were dimly conscious of this difficulty and dimly saw the only possible solution of it, when they maintained that in the co-operative commonwealth every consumer should take his share in the work of producing material commodities. Given the existing psychology of production and consumption, if there is any class which does not contribute to the labour of industrial production, there will always be a danger that such production is not reduced to the minimum compatible with comfort, and that the class that produces will be exploited by the class which consumes but does not produce. It was a recognition of this which led the early co-operators to put forward their ideal of a Co-operative Commonwealth in which the principles of communism were applied both to consumption and to production. The simplest form of this faith is to be found in those small self-contained and self-supporting communities which Owen and his followers vainly attempted to establish. Every member of such a community was to perform an equal share in the work required for the support of the community and would receive an equal share of the products. The attempt failed, because in the industrialized society of Western Europe the small self-supporting community is an impossible anachronism, but the principle and ideal of these pioneers were sound. Socialism and communism are not attainable unless there is a direct and personal correlation between production and consumption (of the necessaries of life), a personal identification of the producer and consumer.

The difficulty is, of course, to find in a highly organized and industrialized society any correlation or any personal identification which will really affect the psychology of either consumption or production. To lay it down merely that everyone must perform a share of industrial production before he is allowed to consume his share of industrial products is not enough. The division of labour is now so minute that any direct relation between any individual's production and consumption will always be extremely rare. The result is that to make every consumer a producer will not necessarily establish any direct relation between the psychology of an individual as consumer with his psychology as producer. It is here, in my opinion, that the Russian Communists have made a mistake. They are right in laying down as a principle of communism that every consumer must also be a producer, but unconsciously they accept the capitalist psychology of production. They organize society in such a way that in effect every consumer has to " work," but the basis of their organization is production or work, not consumption. Russia to-day is organized for " work " or production, and you have a highly centralized system of government in which everyone is set to produce what the Central Government, the apex of the organized producers, considers ought to be produced. It is true that the productive capacity of the community may ultimately in this way be increased and that a juster equilibrium between consumption and production is established over the whole community—a very important achievement. But what commodities shall be produced, and in what quantities, is decided by a bureaucracy. In Russia at the moment that bureaucracy is in effect responsible to no one, and there is considerable evidence to show that it has accepted the capitalist psychology of production in so far as it aims at industrializing

Russia. In this industrialization its ideal is industrial
efficiency in the capitalist sense. The speeches and
writings of Russian Bolsheviks show no sign that they
have got beyond the point of judging production by
the standard of quantity, or of accepting it as right
and natural that the best which great masses of human
beings can hope for is to spend eight hours of their
day all their life long labouring in factories. It may,
of course, be argued that this outlook is temporary,
the result of the blockade and the attacks by capitalist
Governments or of the Bolshevik autocracy.   But
even if Russia had peace and the Soviet system were
really in operation, the control of industry would be
in the hands of a bureaucracy and executive answer-
able only to organized producers, and the Government
and system would therefore reflect the views, not of
consumers, but of the strongest bodies of producers.
There would be no direct relation between the demand
of the individual and community as consumers and
the labour of the individual and community as
producers.

The question which the socialist ought to face is
whether it is possible to establish such a correlation
between consumption and production both in the
machinery and psychology of society. It is quite clear
that it cannot be established fully and directly in the
individual, because under modern conditions no
individual will produce what he consumes or consume
what he produces. The only way, therefore, in which
the correlation could establish itself would be as a
reaction upon the individual through the organization
of industry. I believe that it is possible, though I
admit that it would be very difficult, to achieve this
through the Co-operative Commonwealth. In order to

explain this I must endeavour to put the working of this Commonwealth, as I conceive it, in a somewhat more concrete form before the reader.

The reader must imagine the whole industrial system of the country transferred to the control of the consumers, organized on the model of the existing Co-operative Movement. Every individual would be a member of his local unit or society, and the machinery of the movement, as I have explained in my book, *Co-operation and the Future of Industry*, makes it possible for full democratic control over industry to be exercised, provided only that the democratic spirit exists in the community. Every individual would be required to contribute an approximately equal share of labour necessary for production and would be entitled to an equal share in the products. There would be no great difficulty in adapting the machinery of co-operative industry to the task of estimating the amount of labour required and of apportioning it. The task would be nothing like so difficult as that now performed by a vast capitalist trust in estimating the demand and organizing production to meet that demand. The whole co-operative system makes for an easy and rapid translation of the consumer's demand to the centres of industrial production, and its principle is that demand should create supply rather than supply create demand. It is not, therefore, fantastic to assume that the national body in the Co-operative Commonwealth, answering to what is now the C.W.S. in the Co-operative Movement, could estimate the amount of commodities and services required for any particular year—and therefore the amount of industrial labour required—on the basis of the ascertained demand during the previous

year. Just as the demand for commodities and
services was translated from the individual consumer
up from the local unit or store, through the members'
quarterly meeting, the elected Management Committee, to the national body, the national quarterly
delegate meeting and the national C.W.S. directors,
so the demand for labour to produce the commodities
and services would be translated downwards from the
C.W.S. directors and the delegates' quarterly meeting
through the local unit to the individual consumer.
The consumer who exercised his demand for commodities and services through his local society would
thus find that in return his local society was demanding his labour for the production or provision of those
commodities and services.

Have we in such a system the possibility of a
direct correlation between this demand for products
and the demand for labour? The answer must depend
partly upon the working of the system and partly upon
the motives which may reasonably be expected to
operate under such a system. Let us first examine
the motives which may be expected to operate. If
the co-operative system were co-extensive with the
industry of the country and were no longer struggling
for existence in the middle of a society organized by
and for capitalism, every motive for profit-making,
both in the rank and file of the community and in
its executives, would be eliminated. Every individual
would be called upon by his society to contribute so
much labour per annum, and he would receive from
his society a credit, representing an equal share of the
commodities and services, against which he could
purchase commodities and services during the year.
The dividend upon purchase would be paid to him.

just as it is now in the Co-operative Movement, so that
each consumer would obtain those commodities which
he chose to consume, as his share of the community's
income, at a price which answered to cost of production. The possibility of profit-making would be
eliminated and therefore the motive would decay and
die out. As a consumer, there would be a strong
impulse in the individual to use his power, as a member
of his local society, to get the society to supply what
he wanted to consume. This impulse would be
enormously stronger than it is in the Movement to-day.
To-day the co-operator who cannot get exactly what
he wants at his store can always go and try to get it
at the shop next door. But in the Co-operative
Commonwealth there would be no capitalist shop
round the corner; if the consumer could not get what
he wanted at a store, he would not be able to get it
at all. There would, therefore, be a very strong
motive for the members to insist upon the store supplying what they required. This is exactly what is
desirable, a real and active control by the consumers
over industrial production. Under such a system the
local or national executive which did not supply a
commodity, demanded by any large local or national
section of the consumers, would very soon find itself
turned out and a new executive elected with a mandate
to produce that commodity. At the same time the
fact that the consumer received his share of the
communal income in the form of a money credit
against which he could purchase commodities and
services would ensure that the individual possessed
the widest possible liberty of exercising individual
taste in his consumption, and that the influence of
individual demand across the shop counter was

retained under this co-operative system. There would
be no reason why the consumer should be confined
to purchasing only from the store in his locality;
convenience would ensure that the staple commodities
of household consumption were, as they are to-day,
obtained locally, but if a man living in Kensington
found that he preferred the ties supplied in Peckham,
or a lady living in Peckham found that she preferred
the dresses supplied in Mayfair, there is no reason
why these consumers should not carry their credit
notes to Peckham and Mayfair respectively and make
their purchase there.

Thus this system would ensure that the main impulse
and principle in the production of industrial commodities and the provision of services was the demand
issuing from the community for such commodities and
services as they wanted to consume or use. It would
encourage the exercise of individual and communal
demand and retain even the very real pleasure of
private shopping, but it would give no place or
opportunity for the stimulation of demand from the
centre or by individuals who would profit privately
from the stimulation of such a demand. The question
now has to be considered whether there would also
be a reaction upon the demand from the organization
and sphere of production, which would work in such
a way as to confine the demand to products and
services of obvious utility. I do not believe that this
would happen if there were a sudden and cataclysmic
transition from the society of to-day to the society
of the Co-operative Commonwealth. We are so
accustomed to a society composed of exploiters and
exploited, our minds are so warped by the existing
psychology of production, our taste so corrupted by

a century of scientific capitalistic advertizing, that we should not find in ourselves or in others those social beliefs and desires corresponding to the framework of the fully developed socialist or co-operative society which I have sketched. But if the transition were made gradually, say in one or two generations, so that the crude elements of capitalist psychology were eliminated, then, I think, this method of industrial production and distribution would itself allow and encourage a correlation between industrial production and consumption.

We have seen that there is reason to believe that the co-operative system, developed and universalized, would make one of the main causes of industrial production the demand for goods and services by the consumers. The ideal society would be one in which this demand was only for commodities and services strictly useful, so that industry produced a high standard of material comfort combined with simplicity, and the community and individual were free to devote the greater part of their time and energy to activities other than those of industry. Would there be any motives acting under the system proposed by me which might be expected to make for such conditions? I think there would. The individual would stand in a two-fold relationship to the co-operative industrial organization. As a consumer, he would be a member of his local society, would obtain all the necessaries of life from it, and would in conjunction with other members of his local community exercise in the quarterly meeting a power of determining what products should be produced for him to use or consume. The aggregate of these individual and local communal demands would determine the

aggregate of goods and services which were produced
in the whole community, and, therefore, the amount
of industrial labour necessary in the whole community.
The individual who had exercised his demand as a
consumer in his local society would also find that he
stood in the relation of producer to that society, and
that through it he was called upon to contribute his
share to the aggregate of communal labour. In every
act of his as a member of this industrial organization,
whether in electing the executive or demanding some
commodity or service, this two-fold relationship would
be brought home to him. And it would be brought
home to him in the only way which ensures that the
individual will take an active interest in, and exercise
his right to a share in, democratic control of a complex
organization, namely, by affecting him personally and
vitally in each relationship.

How this would happen may be shown by considering the actual working of the Co-operative Movement
to-day. The relationship of the co-operator to his
Movement is, of course, to-day not dual, he is merely
a consumer, and, even as a consumer, he is not vitally
affected by its operations as he would be if it were
co-extensive with the whole of the country's industry.
Yet again and again at the quarterly meetings of
local societies and of the Wholesale Society you can
see the consumers' demand brought to bear upon the
executive, and the executive forcing the consumer to
consider his demand in relation to factors in production. At a quarterly meeting of a local society you
may find the members pressing the Management
Committee to provide goods of different or better
quality, to start a bakery or milk supply, or to open
a new branch store; at the C.W.S. delegates' meetings

you may find the delegates of societies making the same kind of demands upon the Directors. The Management Committee or Directors will either comply with these demands, or, perhaps, they will reply to the members or delegates : " We are aware of this demand and we realize the desirability of meeting it, but members must understand that the following difficulties or disadvantages attach to the production of this commodity . . ." The decision then rests in the hands of the members; if the demand is sufficiently keen and widespread and they consider that there is a balance of advantage in producing the commodity, they can by a vote instruct their executives to start production.

In a fully developed socialist co-operative system of industry the same process would take place, but far more effectively. If any considerable body of consumers in a locality were dissatisfied with any commodity or service, or demanded a commodity or service not supplied to them, the demand would be raised at the quarterly meeting of the local society, and, if the demand were at all extensive and applied to goods or services not supplied locally, instructions would be given to delegates to raise the question at the C.W.S. meetings. The demand might be capable of satisfaction without adding to the labour of the community, through a slight reorganization of industry or a diversion of labour from the production of one kind of article to that of another. In such a case the executives would have no motive or reason for refusing the demand. But the executives might find that, if they satisfied this demand, they would have to call upon the community for an increased quantity of labour. An increase in labour would affect everyone in the community, while the non-supply of a particular commodity or service would, in most cases, affect only a portion of the community. An executive would, therefore, always feel that its popularity depended even more upon keeping down the quantity of labour demanded from the community than upon the satisfaction of its demands for commodities. The executive, in order to protect itself, would therefore say to the delegates or members : " We can supply this commodity or service if you persist in demanding it. But you or your constituents must understand clearly that, if we do supply it in the coming year, it will entail an increase of approximately so many hours labour for every member of the community. Before we take any steps involving such an increase of labour, we should like to have a mandate from members or societies." The individual would then be forced to consider the relation of his demand for a commodity or service to the amount of labour involved in its production and supply. If the commodity were really and widely desired, and if the increase in labour necessary for its production were not excessive, the consumer's demand would almost certainly prevail; but if these conditions were not fulfilled the producer's view would win and the commodity would not be supplied.

We have here, I submit, the kind of personal correlation between consumption and production, a balancing in the individual's mind between the utility of a product and the labour cost of production, which must be the foundation of any socialist industrial system. It is a direct result of basing industrial organization upon the organized consumers and of then applying the principles of communistic production through the machinery of communistic consumption.

There are certain obvious objections and questions with regard to the system sketched here which must now be considered. Objectors will naturally first raise the question whether such a system would be capable of producing efficiently. The acute reader will have gathered from the previous chapters that personally I would demand from one point of view much more, and from another point of view, much less, from an industrial system than capitalists or the majority of socialists. If by efficient production is meant the production of the vast mass of commodities and services produced under capitalist industry, then I believe and hope that the Co-operative Commonwealth would be inefficient. But if by an efficient industrial system is meant a system which tends continually to reduce industrial labour to a minimum and yet produces a high, if simple, standard of material comfort and convenience, then I believe that the Co-operative Commonwealth would be efficient.

What socialism should aim at is a state of society in which every individual contributes an equal share of labour to industrial production, and yet the amount of labour demanded is such that no individual finds his " occupation " in industrial production. I should consider a socialist society efficient if it required every individual to devote the equivalent of three months to industrial production, and left him nine months out of twelve free to devote himself to other activities. The question is whether our socialist co-operative system might reasonably be expected to achieve this and yet to produce a high standard of comfort. An answer is not capable of absolute proof; all that I can do is to give some reasons for answering the

question affirmatively.   The wastefulness and inefficiency of capitalist industry are obvious.   If all the
labour devoted to inducing a demand for commodities
which can be produced profitably were devoted to
the production of food, clothing, housing, etc.; if the
suppression of individual monopoly and vested interest
allowed full use to be made of electric power, transport, etc.; if local and national organization of industry
were directed not to profit-making, but to labour-
saving and efficiency, there would be an immense
saving in labour without any alteration in the standard
of comfort.   Further, a very great saving would be
effected as soon as industry was confined to the
production of simple and useful commodities.   The
terms are, of course, relative; but it is obvious that
to-day industry attempts to supply things which are
not merely useful and simple, but elaborate and
beautiful and luxurious.   That it is desirable that such
things should be produced in a community, I admit;
but I deny that they ought to be, or probably can
be, produced by industry.   Nearly everyone agrees
that the standard of artistic production and of artistic
taste has degenerated enormously since art was
industrialized, and the failure of industry to produce
beautiful things goes to prove that it is not adapted
to such production.

I would ask the reader, before he rejects my
contention, to look at the whole question in the
following way.   Let him consider first the standard
of material comfort in Europe in 1750 as compared
with that of to-day; let him then consider the potential
productive power and the amount of human labour
required in hand-weaving and large-scale textile
machine industry respectively, in boot making in 1750

and a boot factory in Leicester to-day, in a kneading
machine in a modern bakery and the process of
kneading a loaf by hand, in ploughing and reaping
and threshing in 1750 and the work of the tractor
plough, the reaping machine, and threshing machine
of to-day. Is the rise in the general standard of
comfort, after making allowance for the increase in
population, comparable to the increased power of
production which machines have given to human
beings? It is no exaggeration to say that a man
working for one hour to-day can produce as much
housing, furniture, food, or clothing as in 1750 he
could produce by working 100 hours, and in many
cases his productive powers must have been increased
not a hundred-fold, but thousands-fold. Yet this
enormous increase in potential efficiency is not
reflected in the standard of life and leisure of the
majority of the population. This lamentable failure
is due partly to the wasteful inefficiency of industry
organized on a basis of competition for private profit,
partly to the debased standard in consumption which
is fostered by gross inequality in the distribution of
wealth, and partly to the system of advertisement
which is a direct consequence of organizing production
not for use, but for profit-making. And now let the
reader imagine the whole of this potential productive
and labour-saving power directed to a single end.
namely, the supply of goods and services of general
utility at a minimum expenditure of human labour.
I cannot believe that it is optimistic to hold that,
given such conditions, the community could easily
obtain a standard of life a hundred times higher than
that of 1750 with one-fourth the expenditure of labour
upon industrial production which we tolerate to-day.

The first impulse of many people will be to answer that the motive to efficiency which is so strong to-day will not operate under the system which I have sketched. My answer is that it depends entirely upon what is meant by efficiency. Industry to-day is extremely efficient in producing things which can be sold at a profit and at inducing the majority to buy things which the minority sells at a profit; it has failed absolutely to produce things which will both raise the general standard of comfort and reduce the aggregate volume of human labour. But under our socialist co-operative system there would always be powerful motives operating to create the latter kind of efficiency. Let us take a concrete example. Suppose a demand from the consumers for some commodity or service pressed upon the C.W.S. at a delegate meeting, and a reply from the directors that it would be quite possible to supply it, but that it would entail so many hours extra labour per individual. In such a case, if it were possible by a reorganization of industry on more efficient lines to supply the commodity or service without increasing the amount of labour, there would immediately arise an agitation for the reorganization, for everyone would gain and no one would lose by the adoption of the more efficient method. The demand would probably originate from those members of the community who were actually engaged in producing the commodity and were familiar with the conditions of production, and, once the possibility of more economical and efficient production were proved, the demand for reorganization would be irresistible. Take, for instance, the obviously immense possibilities of increased efficiency and of labour saving in the centralization of electric power

to be applied to industry. Whether such possibilities
are exploited to-day depends almost entirely upon the
question of reconciling the private interests of a few
capitalists and companies, and efficiency is sacrificed,
because, though it would pay the community, vested
interests would suffer and the profits of a minority
might decline.   Under the socialist co-operative
system the demand for this reorganization would be
irresistible, because not a single member of the
community would lose and every member would gain
by an increase in efficiency of production.   Under
such a system there would, in fact, be from every
side and continually a strong demand for efficiency,
efficiency in the sense of the greatest possible reduction
of the human effort involved in industrial production.
And since no class or individual in the whole community would have anything to gain, would, in fact,
lose, by resisting this demand, we might legitimately
expect to see an increase of this kind of efficiency
which to-day would be inconceivable.

The great revolutions in human history have come
from small and often obscure causes which have
helped to channel the motives, desires, and beliefs of
vast numbers of people in a given direction.   The
motive of profit-making has probably always existed
in human beings, but the discovery that steam would
move a steel rod backwards and forwards led directly
to the channelling of this motive until it became the
most universal and perhaps the strongest of all the
streams in individual and social psychology. Affection
for the locality where one has been born or where one
lives, and the ties of a common language, tradition,
and life, have for many hundreds of years been part
of the psychology of most human beings; then

obscure historical causes connected with the cutting
off of a king's head by the proletariat of Paris led
quite suddenly to the channelling of these feelings,
beliefs, and aspirations, until vast masses of men, all
moved now by the same motives and aims, were
swept along by the great current of modern
nationalism to overturn thrones and States and
Governments and boundaries, to free themselves and
enslave other people, to attain inconceivable heights
of heroism and self-sacrifice and inconceivable depths
of barbarity and savagery, to slaughter one another
by millions, and, in the name of nationality and
civilization, to destroy the national civilization of
Europe. So, too, the channelling of those common
beliefs and motives which constitute the demand of
the consumer and the psychology of the industrial
producer, so that they would all act in the direction
of industrial efficiency, would probably revolutionize
society by increasing production and reducing the
human effort required in production.

What standard of material comfort would be produced by industry organized on these communal lines,
and with all the interests of both consumer and
producer making for industrial efficiency, must be a
matter of conjecture. I am quite willing to put it
low, as low as the standard which now exists in the
most advanced industrial community. I have argued
and assumed in these pages that industry will be
confined to the production of useful commodities and
services. And at first the whole tendency of the
system would make for limiting industry to the
production of necessaries and necessary luxuries,
because the industrial machinery, when first taken
over by the Co-operative Commonwealth, would still

be organized, not for the efficient production of things required by the community, but for the production of things which can be sold at a profit. The amount of labour demanded from the individual would therefore in the first years be high, and the return in commodities and services low, and this would make for a demand from the community for a decrease in labour and a simpler standard of consumption. Many people will consider this to be an objection; to me it seems an immense merit. The demand would show itself concretely as a demand that labour should be reduced by the simplification of production. We should then probably eat simpler food, wear simpler clothes, live in simpler houses, and use simpler furniture. I do not believe that we should be any the less comfortable, and I am sure that our cities and houses and homes would be infinitely more beautiful than they are to-day. The things which we used, from our chairs and door-knockers and mantel-pieces to our watches and electric torches and knives and forks, would be made simply and solely with a view to use; all the elaborate and hideous traditional ornamentation, which you can observe, if you like, in the mantel-piece, fire-place, and coal-scuttle in your own room, would disappear. Let the man who reads this compare the articles which I have just mentioned with the spade and rake which he uses in his back garden : the garden tools are, by convention, made only for use; their shape is extraordinarily traditional, but the tradition is solely that of simplicity and use. The shape and ornamentation of the mantel-piece, etc., are also conventional, but the convention is here not that it shall be made solely for use, but that it shall " look nice " in the room. And now I would ask anyone

to try and look at a mantel-piece and a spade as if
he had never seen either of them before, as if he had
never learnt that elaborate black scrolls and circles
and leaves, and wood carved into patterns, and a tile
with a blue ship on it, were necessarily beautiful; if
he does this, I think he will allow that a spade or
a rake or a garden fork has a satisfactoriness and
beauty of its own which can compare very favourably
with the elaborately ornamented poker or coal-scuttle
or mantel-piece. And the saving of labour in simplicity, as compared with ornamentation, can be
estimated from the relative cheapness of the simple
agricultural implement, designed solely for use, as
compared with the elaborately ornamented shovel,
poker, and tongs which disfigure our hearths.

In order to avoid misunderstanding, I may say that
I do not believe or advocate what many people mean
by "the simple life." The more comfortable people
are, the happier and better they are, and neither
simplicity nor discomfort has any merit in itself. I
should prefer to see the whole world dressed in silks
and satins than in sack-cloth; but on the other hand,
a world in which everyone had to dress in broad-cloth
would be a better place than one in which large
numbers had to dress in sack-cloth in order that a
few might have silks and satins. I see no reason,
indeed, why a socialist co-operative system might not,
by efficient organization of industry, in time produce
a general standard of material comfort such as we
should regard to-day as luxurious; but our taste, as
consumers, is to-day so corrupted by commercialism,
industrialism, and class-snobbery, that it could only
be cured by a period during which conditions of
production concentrated the efforts of producers and

consumers upon simplicity and utility in products. I
do not believe, as I have said before, that even in
the first years of a Co-operative Commonwealth the
real standard of material comfort would be inferior
to that of the present time. Nine-tenths of the commodities which people now consider necessary to their
comfort will be found, upon examination, in no way
to make them comfortable, and often positively to
make them uncomfortable. They are really commodities which commercialism and industrialism have
induced people to believe that they want to buy, and
the motive for buying them is usually convention or
class-snobbery. The houses of the rich and the
innumerable unsightly objects which encumber them
seem, indeed, designed to make their inhabitants
uncomfortable but, at the same time, to make it
unmistakable that their inhabitants are rich and
belong to a certain class. In most houses the most
comfortable room is the kitchen, and it is a significant
fact that large numbers of people habitually live in
their kitchens, though they keep a sitting room in
which they receive visitors. The sitting room is the
most expensively furnished room in the house and
also the most uncomfortable, because it and its
furniture are not designed for use, but in order to
prove to the world that the inhabitants have a certain
income and the ornaments and curtains which go with
respectability.

The world would not lose much if industry in the
Co-operative Commonwealth produced simpler and
fewer commodities than it does to-day. In its early
years conditions would tend to restrict production to
those commodities and services which the community
considered most useful. Utility and use would be the

main standards in industrial production. We should still manufacture industrially footballs, books, newspapers, electric torches, and bicycles, as well as food, clothes, and furniture, but we should no longer attempt to make any of these things beautiful. I have said, with some hesitation, in a previous chapter that I believe that industrial production is probably unsuitable for producing beautiful objects or objects good in themselves. It is obvious that the statement is true, given the existing psychology of production and consumption. That is why it seems to me important that in the early years of the socialist co-operative system industry should be applied only to the production of articles which are useful, and that no attempt should be made to make them beautiful. The principal aim of the community would be to produce industrially a large number or great quantities of commodities of practical utility, and at the same time to reduce the amount of industrial labour required from the community. This, however, would not mean that there would be no production of beautiful things; they would certainly be produced, only they would not be produced by industry. If every individual had nine months of the year free of " work," and if he had assured for himself, by his three months' work, a sufficiency of food, clothing, housing, and material comforts, large numbers of persons would undoubtedly feel an impulse to spend some part of their free time in producing things which were not useful to meet their own and other people's demand. Art, literature, music, science, learning, the drama, recreations, would thus be completely divorced from industrialism and commercialism, and, since for the first time in the world's history the whole community would have the leisure necessary for their development and enjoyment, one might look for an outburst of scientific and artistic activity, and a conentration of effort upon activities which make for a humane and pleasurable existence, such as the ferocious human herd has never previously known.

I do not pretend to be able, nor do I wish, to lay down exactly the lines upon which such a socialist co-operative society must develop. What I maintain is that the growth of a vicious communal psychology of production and consumption makes essential a period during which there will be a complete divorce between the productive industrial activities and other activities of the community. As I conceive it, the community during that period would be organized co-operatively, in the manner sketched in the previous pages, for the production of material commodities and the services necessary for a comfortable existence. The vast mass of the population would for the first time find itself released from the struggle for bare existence, and the motive of economic competition, which is not a necessary or natural ingredient in human society, would gradually fade out. And at the same time that the masses found themselves freed from this economic struggle and assured the necessaries of a comfortable material existence, they would also obtain an enormous increase in leisure. It is, of course, possible that that leisure would be misused. It is possible that the community would still demand the production of hideous and useless objects and would spend its leisure in their production; it is possible that it would spend its leisure in drink and in debauchery. But there is no real ground for such pessimism. If the conditions which now create the

motives of the economic struggle for existence, of
economic competition and profit-making, of class-
snobbery, were removed, I believe that there would
immediately arise an enormous demand for and supply
of those things which make for a humane communal
life. After all, even to-day most people, when they get
a little leisure, spend it in pursuing a hobby, in going to
a play or cinema, in playing or watching games, in
reading, in educating themselves, or merely in enjoy-
ing themselves. It is the class structure of modern
society and the pressure of the economic war and
competition which are the great enemies of individual
development in these non-economic activities. The
abolition of this class structure and economic war
would give the individual free scope for the development of these activities. There would, I believe, be
an enormous demand for education, for books, plays,
cinemas, games and sports, music, etc. Voluntary
associations on a non-economic basis for a supply of
these things would spring up, just as to-day among
the small class which has leisure voluntary associations
are continually coming into existence, not for the
purpose of making money, but to supply the demand
for lawn tennis or discussion or dancing or scientific
research or private theatricals or horticulture.

The institution of this system would, for the reasons
which I have indicated, produce a profound change
in the individual and communal psychology of production and consumption. The change would be so
profound that it would be foolish to speculate upon
its ultimate effects in society. One conjecture may
however be allowed. Once the system were fully
developed it would make for a great increase in
industrial efficiency and would encourage in the

community a very high standard of values in consumption.   The interaction of these two conditions
might eventually make society ripe for a further social
revolution.   The time might come when scientific
discovery and organization rendered industry so
efficient that the production of the material basis for
comfortable existence made only a negligible demand
upon the time and labour of the individuals who are
comprised in the community.   At the same time the
sense of values or the taste of the community, its
power of distinguishing the useful from the useless,
the beautiful from the ugly, the good from the bad,
would have become extraordinarily active and delicate
compared to what they are to-day.   A civilized
community of that kind might be able to apply
industry to the production of commodities other than
the necessaries of life by methods and in forms which
we, with our false standards and perverted taste, could
not even dimly imagine.   But it is as useless for us
to speculate about the future of a civilized man as it
would have been for our ape-like ancestor in primeval
forests to speculate as to the future of his uncivilized
human descendant.

Two other points, which will probably have arisen
as objections to these speculations in the minds of
many readers, remain to be dealt with.   The first is
a question of the organization of labour under this
socialist co-operative system.   Many people will object
to any system which rests ultimately upon compulsion,
and I agree that compulsion is always an evil.   But,
with the existing social psychology, no social system
is conceivable which would not somewhere contain an
element of compulsion, either direct or indirect.   The
whole machinery of the existing capitalist society is

so arranged as to compel the majority of the population to work at a particular trade for a given wage by
the threat of starvation. Direct compulsion by the
State, in the shape of legal enactments against com-
bination on the part of the workers and laws like the
Emergency Powers Act, has been in the past and is
to-day being applied wherever possible. But no
socialist system which has been devised as a practical
alternative to capitalism really dispenses with an
element of compulsion. The Russian communists
immediately adopted and applied a system of direct
and indirect compulsion. A Guild Socialist society
would rest ultimately upon the kind of indirect compulsion which exists to-day, for the vast mass of the
population, if it did not join and labour in some Guild,
would just be starved to death. The question whether
this kind of indirect starvation compulsion or direct
legal compulsion is preferable, is, I find, very difficult
to answer. When in the year before the Russian
revolution I wrote *Co-operation and the Future of
Industry*, I was inclined to believe that it would be
better to give to the economic organization of society
a legal power to call upon the individual to perform
his share of industrial production. Since then many
different events have shown the danger of concentrat-
ing legal powers of compulsion in any part of an
organized community, and I feel far less inclined to
dogmatize to-day than I did in 1917. The matter is,
however, of no very great importance, for the socialist
co-operative system would work with or without direct
compulsion. In the first case, the community of
consumers, having received a legal monopoly of industrial production, would also receive legal powers to
call upon each member of the community to perform

an equal share of labour in that production, and each individual would then obtain a right to an equal share in the products. But, as a matter of fact, if the community of organized consumers retained in its hands the monopoly of industrial production and made the right to a share in the products contingent upon the performance of labour, the use of direct legal compulsion would be unnecessary. The same sort of starvation compulsion, which exists to-day and would exist under Guild Socialism, would also operate in this case. The individual who refused to answer the call of the community to perform his share of production would find himself debarred from any share, as a consumer, in the products of industry. A very few persons might, by cunning or fraud, take advantage of this system and escape their obligations, but the need for food and clothing, and all the other necessaries of life, would indirectly compel the vast majority to fulfil their obligations.

The second objection is one which has often been raised against those who look to co-operation as a real alternative to the capitalist system. The field of industry, it is said, in which the Co-operative Movement has proved successful is extremely limited; it has succeeded hitherto only in those departments of industry which supply the demand for commodities "of personal or domestic consumption"; it has not proved itself capable of extending its operations to the major industries, to those industries, e.g., mining or machine making, which supply commodities not to the individual consumer, but to other industries, or to transport; and it is argued or assumed that these limitations are inherent in the co-operative system. I have dealt, in *Co-operation and the Future of*

Industry, with this objection and with the possibilities
of extension in the Co-operative Movement; I do not
propose to repeat here what I wrote in that book, but
only to supplement it. The view that co-operation
is incapable or unsuitable of application to the whole
field of industrial production, though desirable and
possible in a limited field, seems to me to be due to
misunderstanding and confusion. Both Mr. Cole and
Mr. and Mrs. Webb, who tend to take this view,
confuse the existing Movement with the system of
co-operative industry. The Movement, as it exists
to-day, is an organization of the economically weak
elements in society who are in revolt against the
tyranny of the strongest elements, the capitalists, and
their whole system. It is competing against the
capitalist system on ground chosen by the capitalist
whom it found already in possession. You cannot
assume that a limitation in the operations of the
existing Movement is due to something inherent in
the co-operative system; it may simply be due to the
weakness of its economic position in the centre of a
capitalist system. Again, it may be true that merely
by competing against the capitalist on his own ground
the co-operators will never, because of the weak
economic position from which they started, be able
to oust the capitalist from the whole field of industry.
But no Guild Socialist, like Mr. Cole, or State and
Municipal Socialists, like Mr. and Mrs. Webb, believe
that either Guild Socialism or State Socialism could
be successfully established over the whole field of
industry by allowing these systems to compete with
the capitalist system on its own ground. Mr. Cole
looks to a revolution or to legislation to give a
monopoly of industrial production to the Guilds, and

Mr. and Mrs. Webb would give a legal monopoly to the
State or the Municipality. So, too, with the co-
operative system; what we have to ask ourselves is
whether that system is the best for controlling
industry and is capable of application to the whole of
industry, and, if we answer the question affirmatively,
then we should adopt every possible method, including
legislation, of placing the whole of industry in the
hands of the community of consumers organized on
the co-operative system.

This book has argued so far that the co-operative
is the most rational system for the control of industry,
but I still have to answer the question whether it is
capable of application to every department of
industry. With regard to this I must confine myself
to asking the reader to consider the following points.
The co-operative system, about which we are talking,
is a method of organizing the community, in their
capacity of consumers, in local units or societies, and
of federating those local units in national bodies. The
ownership of the instruments of production and the
control of industry are then vested in these organs and
so in the community. The individuals, organized in
their units, elect representatives or executives to carry
on, under their general control, the day-to-day
management of industry. The essential feature of this
system is that the individual is organized solely as
a consumer of industrial commodities or of services,
and that the dividend on purchase eliminates the
possibility of profit-making by one class at the expense
of another. We know that this system works : it is
working to-day distributively or locally in the store,
and nationally in the large-scale distribution and
production of the Wholesale Societies. No one has

ever advanced any positive reason to show that such a system is not capable of indefinite extension to any and every form of industrial production, and, as a matter of fact, it is self-evident that it is capable.

Let us take, as an example, the case of the national railway service which, according to Mr. and Mrs. Webb, could not be controlled co-operatively, but could be controlled by the State. " The national railway service," they write, " could hardly be governed by the votes of the incoherent mob of passengers who pour out of the termini of our great cities; or the characteristic municipal services by any other membership than that of all the municipal electors." This passage shows a curious misconception of the whole problem of socialist, democratic, and co-operative control of industry. The first half of the sentence is not an argument against co-operative control of the transport industry; it merely points to a fact which indicates a general difficulty of applying democratic or socialistic control to any railway system. The users of railways are, in fact, the whole community, and the problem is to organize the community in such a way that it controls the railway system in the interests of the community of users. The co-operative system would organize the community, not as a mob of people issuing from a railway station— it does not organize its own members to-day as a mob of people issuing from the doors of a crowded store—but as a number of individual consumers residing in particular localities. That, too, is what a system of nationalization or municipalization attempts to do, but in a much more confused and inefficient manner. When you nationalize the railways, you take the mob of consumers (which issues from the

termini), divide them up into parliamentary constituencies, allow them to elect representatives, and place
the administration of the railways in the hands of
the elected representatives.   That is precisely what
the co-operative system would do; the only difference
between the two systems would be that under nationalization the representatives are elected not specifically
to represent the community of consumers and to
administer industrial undertakings, but for every sort
and kind of political, moral, and economic purpose
which may fall within the purview of Parliament.
The same is also true of municipalization.

In a fully developed socialist society, therefore, the
railways, trams, and mines would be " nationalized "
or " municipalized," but they would be handed over
to the control, not of the political, parliamentary, or
municipal organization, but to a co-operative national
or municipal organization.   Once more I do not wish
to dogmatize as to details; I will merely hazard a
guess as to the general outline of the organization.
Parliament and the municipalities as we know them
would remain, the national and local representative
bodies of men and women in their general capacity
of citizens.   Their functions would be political and co-
ordinative, in the strictest sense legislative.   For that
very reason they are and would be unsuited for the
control of industry, for representing the interests of
the community as consumers of industrial products
and the users of industrial services.   The function of
controlling industry, whether of administering a
railway service or of supplying bread, would be
delegated to an organization or organizations, local
and national, of consumers, established on the co-
operative system.   I have said " or organizations "

because it might in practice be found advisable to have a separate organization for the control of transport, power, etc., from that which controlled the production and distribution of other commodities; but the point is not of any real importance. The really important point is that the individual, organized as a consumer in the locality where he lives, would elect representatives specifically for the economic purpose of providing the goods and services. It would be quite possible for the whole of industry to be controlled by a single consumers' organization, the division of labour being carried out within the organization itself. In that case the consumer would go to the quarterly meeting of his local consumers' unit (answering to the existing local society) and elect a local management committee or committees. He would elect on to that committee or committees representatives to control and manage the business of supplying the commodities required for his personal consumption, other representatives to control the tram and omnibus services, others again the national transport services or the lighting and heating services. The local units or consumers' organizations would be federated regionally and nationally, in accordance with the requirements of industrial organization, just as the co-operative societies of to-day are federated. Thus the railways would be managed by a national Board, composed of delegates from districts or regions and drawn from those members of local management committees who were specifically elected by the individual consumers to represent them as users of railways. So, too, the tramways and omnibus services of London would be managed by a Board, composed of delegates from the local consumers' units of the London area who had been specifically elected to the local management committees to represent the individual consumers as users of local systems of communication.

This developed co-operative organization may appear to be complicated when described in general terms. It is, however, simple when compared to the existing system or to any of the alternatives proposed by socialists. Compare it, for instance, to the hopelessly confused and complicated organization under which we now live, with its thousands of joint stock companies, each of which is a little clique of capital-owning people who elect a management committee to control some corner of the field of industry in their own interests and against the interests of the rest of the community. Or compare it to the proposed system of the State socialist who would ask us, once in four or five or seven years, to go and elect a representative who is to represent us as a user of mines, railways, power, and an infinite number of other commodities, and also to continue to represent us for all the heterogeneous purposes for which we are now supposed to elect a Member of Parliament. Or compare it with the extraordinarily complicated system of Guild Socialism as described by a writer like Mr. Cole in his book, *Guild Socialism Restated*, in which there is an amazing pullulation of Guilds, Co-operative organizations, Collective Utilities Councils, Cultural Councils, Health Councils, Communes, and in which the " good life " of society and the individual is made to depend upon an infinite series of elections and upon the astonishing assumption that water-tight groups of producers, possessing an absolute monopoly in the various departments of industry, will suddenly shed the psychology of capitalist production and accept that of social service.

The co-operative system is of universal applicability, because like the capitalist system, it is based upon a social philosophy. Its elasticity may be shown by one last example, and the reader will, perhaps, pardon me if I give it in the form of a personal reminiscence. About seven years ago the Fabian Research Department instituted an enquiry into "The Control of Industry," and the report on the possibilities of the Co-operative Movement was drafted by Mr. and Mrs. Webb. They argued confidently against the practicability of the co-operative system extending its operations to various parts of the field of industry, and among other limitations they mentioned that of international trade, holding that "the bulk of the production and dealing for export is beyond the range of the Co-operative Movement." The report was considered at a Fabian Summer School, and I was asked to open the discussion. I argued, as I have done in this book, that the co-operative system was applicable to the whole of industry, and was, in fact, the most practicable method of applying socialistic principles to international trade. I failed entirely to convince either the writers of the report or the other Fabians. But events have succeeded where I failed. In the following passage from Mr. and Mrs. Webb's last book, *A Constitution for the Socialist Commonwealth of Great Britain*, they show the feasibility of extending the co-operative system to international trade, using precisely the same arguments as those with which I failed to convince them in 1913 :

"The critics of the Co-operative Movement are always pointing out that the very origin and

purpose of Democracies of Consumers is production
for use and not for exchange, and it is to this all-
important characteristic that they owe alike their
practical success and their theoretical justification.
That being the case, is not the Co-operative Movement, or for that matter, any Democracy of
Consumers, obligatory as well as voluntary, con-
clusively debarred from manufacturing and trading
in goods to be bought and consumed not by their
own members, but by non-members inhabiting other
countries, and living under other governments?
Recent developments have, however, discovered
that Democracies of Consumers, far from being
limited to the supply of their own members, may
be found to be the one and only solution of international trade on Socialistic principles, independent
either of the capitalist importer or exporter, or
both of them.   Thus the Co-operative Wholesale
Societies of half a dozen European countries, besides
themselves obtaining directly from abroad an
increasing part of the supplies that they severally
require, have begun to exchange with each other
their surplus products or those for which they
possess exceptional advantages.   And during the
Great War nearly all the Governments themselves
acted as collectivist importers on a gigantic scale,
purchasing abroad—often directly from other
Governments—not only every kind of munitions,
but also enormous quantities of metals, wool,
cotton, wheat, meat and other requirements of
their own people.   To the extent to which either of
these movements develops, the export trade of the
world, conducted by capitalist merchants for private
profit, will have been transformed essentially into

a reciprocal exchange of imports, conducted by paid
agents of the consumers and citizens, to the
exclusion of capitalist profit. There seems no reason
why this demonstrably practicable ' collectivization
of international trade '—in which the Co-operative
Movement would play an ever-increasing part—
should not become the predominant form between
civilized communities. In a world in which all
industry was socialized, all speculative exporting
for private profit would cease : in its stead there
would be reciprocal imports, organized by Democracies of Consumers for use instead of for exchange.
And seeing that the Democracies of Consumers
(whether they take the form of Co-operative Movements or of nationalized or municipalized industries)
of one country might become constituent members
of similar bodies in all other countries, there would
cease to be any production for exchange or any
' profit on price.' The whole world would become
one vast complicated network of associations of
consumers, starting from different centres, penetrating continents and traversing oceans, without
exploiting for private profit either the faculties or
the needs of any section of the human race."

Human beings have achieved far more difficult feats
of social organization than the establishment of a
Co-operative Commonwealth of consumers, as sketched
in these pages. I claim that such a Commonwealth
would be practical, rational, human, and humane.
But I am not so foolish as to believe that these are
reasons for its establishment. One requires to read
but little history in order to learn that in the mass
man is neither rational nor human nor humane. Any-

one who has watched the habits of wild beasts in an
Asiatic jungle knows that their communal life is
infinitely more rational and humane than that of the
human packs which have made their lairs in and
around the jungles of London, Paris, and Berlin. In
this book I am " advocating " nothing as rational
or practicable. That is not what I conceive to be
the function of the writer on human society, for, if
it were, he would have to assume that men and
women are influenced by reason. His function is not
advocacy or persuasion, but scientific analysis. He is
a scientist who has performed his task when he can
say : " If you do this that will follow, and if you
want to produce that you must first do this." And
he will always remember that very few people will
accept the facts which his science has proved, and
that no one will act upon them.

CHAPTER V.

THE TRANSITION TO SOCIALISM.

In the previous chapter I attempted to arrive by analysis at the conditions which must exist if the ideals of socialism are to be attained and if a fully developed socialist society is to be a reality. The immediate problem before both the socialist and the co-operator is a practical one; it consists in finding the right methods of passing from the capitalist organization and psychology of the world in which we are living to the socialist organization and psychology of a Co-operative Commonwealth. The problems of this transition period will necessarily, in some respects, be different from those with which I was dealing in the last chapter. If we accept the conclusions of that chapter, we shall not attempt, perhaps, by a cataclysmic revolution, to break up the whole framework of our existing society and establish upon its ruins a brand new consumers' commonwealth; rather we shall seek the right means to develop the existing Co-operative Movement, to oust capitalist control from industry, to encourage the growth of that psychology of consumption and production without which it is hopeless to expect a civilized society. It would be possible to fill many pages with these practical speculations, but the object of this book is rather to establish broad principles than to enquire into the details of organization or political propaganda. I shall, therefore, in this chapter confine myself to a very brief discussion of the main problems which confront the socialist and co-operator in the period of transition.

Our main purpose must be the transfer of the ownership of the instruments of industrial production and the control of industry from the capitalist and capitalist company to the community of consumers, organized co-operatively, in such a way that the transfer is accompanied by a growth of socialist psychology of production and consumption. The impetus to this transfer must, of course, come from the anti-capitalist classes, in other words, from the workers and the co-operators. The co-operator has two tasks before him, neither of which he has hitherto taken up with sufficient energy and seriousness. He has to work for the utmost possible extension of co-operative industry, with the explicit intention of converting his Movement into the instrument by which the community, organized as consumers, may control the whole of industry. He will, however, not succeed in this by his own unaided efforts, or if he does not throw off that parochialism which still clings to him and to his Movement. In other words, he must see that the rank and file of the Movement realize the ideals and principles of co-operation which I have examined in the previous pages; he must envisage his organization not as a little private property nor as a convenient savings bank, but as the embryo of a new world. And it is not enough that he should realize this himself, he must make other people realize it. He must go outside the circle of his quarterly meeting or education committee, and must enlist in his crusade for a new world all those forces which are in revolt against the economic anarchy of capitalism.

The Movement, if it understood its own principles and stood resolutely by them, ought to have the whole of Labour and Socialism solidly behind it.   Nine-tenths of the population are more remorselessly exploited by the present system, as consumers, than they are as producers, and the real charge against capitalism is this exploitation of the community of consumers in the interests of a small minority.

The Movement has an opportunity which, if it be missed, will probably never occur again.   The war has shaken not only the material foundations of the old economic system, but also the acquiescence of masses of men in the moral and mental assumptions upon which it was based.   There has grown up a wide-spread, if vague, consciousness that there is something wrong in an industrial system which works elaborately to exploit the consumers, who are the whole community, in the interests of small minorities.   The agitation against " profiteering " and the movement of public opinion which necessitated rationing in all countries were both symptoms of a revolt among consumers. The Co-operative Movement, with its four million members, alone stands to-day for the principle of a rational organization of industry on a basis of consumption or use.   If its leaders display initiative and imagination, and if they have behind them the under-standing and support of the rank and file, they have an opportunity of appealing successfully to masses of men and women to whom for the first time the shocks of the last six years have brought an active discontent with the irrational injustice and inefficiency of the existing system.

I do not propose to enter into details as to the methods by which an extension of co-operative

industry can be obtained.   But co-operators and
socialists must realize that there are two main
methods.   The Movement can expand by voluntary
association as it has done in the past.   Its success
will depend very greatly upon propaganda of its
principles and ideals.   If there is any truth in the
contentions of my previous chapters, the Movement
ought to have the active assistance of the whole
Labour and Socialist Movement in this propaganda,
and, if that assistance were forthcoming, there ought
to be a vast increase in the membership of the Movement and a rapid extension of industry organized co-
operatively.   But there are obvious limits upon such
developments.   The socialist must also consider an
alternative method of development.   I have argued
throughout this book that the co-operative system
implies, as its logical end, an organization of the whole
community as consumers for the control of industry.
Such an organization can be effected at any time by
legislation.   The whole or any part of industry can,
if the community so desires, be transferred to the
community organized as consumers on co-operative
lines.   It follows from everything which I have said
in the previous pages that, in my opinion, the co-
operator and socialist should take every opportunity
to effect this transfer.

This   immediately   raises   important   practical
questions for the socialist or even for a Labour Party.
It raises, for instance, the whole question of the
relations of co-operation and the Co-operative Movement to proposals for nationalization or municipalization.   I have argued in the previous chapters that in
a fully developed socialist commonwealth the control
of mines or railways or the milk supply should not

be in the hands of the community organized politically (nationalization or municipalization), but in the hands of the community organized as the consumers of the products or services of those industries.   But the socialist wishes to-day to transfer ownership and control in these industries to the community, and he wishes to do so by legislation, i.e., by giving to the organized community a legal monopoly in those industries.   What is to be the immediate programme of a socialist or of a Labour Government?   Are they to hand over these industries to the State or municipality, or are they to attempt to hand them over at once to organizations of consumers?

Most members of the Labour Party, the majority of socialists, and even many co-operators, would answer this question at once in favour of the State and municipality.   Nationalization and municipalization are traditionally inscribed on the Labour programme and are now accepted automatically.   But if the thesis of this book has any truth in it, that attitude requires careful revision.   The objections to placing the control of industry in the hands of the political organs of State and municipality are just as cogent, or rather are more cogent, to-day than they would be in a fully developed socialist society.   The individual acts and votes with regard to Parliament and the municipality not as a consumer of industrial commodities, but as a complex political animal.   At certain stated intervals he goes to a polling booth and votes for a representative, not of himself as a con-sumer, but for all kinds and sorts of political motives and objects.   Having voted, he has finished his political activities and surrendered his power of control until the next election.   There is no quarterly meeting of municipality or State to which the individual can go as a consumer and speak and vote and bring his demand as a consumer into direct relationship with the control of production. The complex organization of the State and municipality, however efficient it might be, can never result in an organization of industry on a basis of consumption or use, and, therefore, nationalization and municipalization will actually prevent the growth of that psychology of consumption and production which will alone make a transition to socialism possible. There are, too, to-day dangers in municipalization and nationalization which would not exist in a society in which industry had already been generally socialized. Most socialists in this country contemplate no sudden and complete expropriation of capitalism, but a gradual municipalization and nationalization. The principle of communal ownership and control is to be introduced piecemeal; a beginning is to be made by handing over the mines and railways to the State, and the milk supply and trams and omnibuses to the municipality, and after that we may, perhaps, go on to expropriate the bankers or shipowners. The danger of this method is that you hand over the control of small pieces of the industrial field to a machine and to political organs dominated by capitalists and the psychology of capitalism. To-morrow you may have a socialist Government which will nationalize the mines or a socialist Borough Council which may municipalize the milk supply; a year later, for no reason connected with industry, the socialist Government or Council may be turned out and capitalists and financiers sit in their places. Does any socialist, who knows the history of municipal graft and the part which " interests " play in a capitalist Parliament, believe that under such circumstances these capitalists and financiers are going to administer the mines or milk supply according to those principles of socialism which we have examined in the preceding pages?

This question is already becoming an urgent and practical one. With a Labour majority in many municipalities, the socialist is actually considering the municipalization of, say, the milk supply. But to municipalize the milk supply means in many places actually to oust the co-operative system, for a considerable number of societies supply milk. It follows from everything that has been said in this book that in such cases a policy of municipalization is directly opposed to the principles and objects of socialism. Where a co-operative system is already applied to milk supply or any other branch of industry in a locality, and where it is capable of extension so as to supply the needs of all the consumers, the right course is to hand over, by legislation, the whole control of that industry to the consumers organized in the existing co-operative system. The proposal to hand over to a co-operative society the whole milk supply of a town will raise an outcry from capitalists, who will say that you are giving a monopoly to a section of the community. You would, of course, be doing nothing of the sort : every consumer of milk would, in so far as he was a consumer of milk, be a member of the society, of the organ of the whole community of consumers ; as a member he would speak and vote at the quarterly meeting ; and, since he would draw his dividend on his purchase of milk, no single person in that town would make a profit out of the milk supply. In other words, all that would have happened would be that, so far as the milk supply of that town was concerned, a voluntary association would have developed, as in fact it has developed in Bale, into the organ of the whole community of organized consumers for the distribution of milk.

Wherever it is possible, the socialist, co-operator, or Labour Party should aim at a transfer of industry to the consumers' organization of the Movement rather than to the political organs of State and municipality. There remain, however, a large number of cases in which, at the present moment, the Movement is, or appears to be, not yet in a position to take over the industry. For instance, practically everyone, even the most convinced' co-operator, would say that the Movement could not take over the mines. What, then, is to be the attitude of the socialist towards the mines? Is he to work for nationalization, for the transfer of this industry to the political organs of the State or to the joint control of State and workers? Most socialists answer this question unhesitatingly in the affirmative; they will condemn what I am going to say as chimerical, yet I would ask the reader, before joining in the condemnation, to consider my contentions with an open mind and in the light of my previous chapters.

I agree that nationalization in the ordinary sense, or joint control of the State or workers, or the kind of semi-socialization which has been applied to the mining industry in Germany, are all preferable to undiluted capitalism. A socialist should probably support any scheme of communal ownership and control as against the present system, not because it would work better or immediately produce a more socialistic society—it is doubtful whether it would—

but because any breach in the walls of capitalism will probably make the transition to a civilized society more easy. Anyone with eyes in his head can see that capitalist society is already dying of auto-intoxication, of the poisons of exploitation, injustice, and class hatred which it inevitably secretes in its own system. If it does not die a violent and sudden death it will sink slowly into a condition of corrupt and lethargic decay. If then it is only a question between private ownership and nationalization, I would always vote for nationalization. But the question can never be as simple and straight-cut as that. If a great industry like mining has to be transferred from private to communal ownership and control, it would always be necessary to create a considerable machinery and organization for its control. If you nationalize the mines to-morrow you have to create a public department, or what answers to a public department, to administer the mines; if you hand them over to the workers you have to create the organization of the Guild; if you do even the little that they have done in Germany you have to create your Coal Council of the Realm and your Coal Association of the Realm. Now it would be just as easy to create this organization on the lines of the co-operative system as on those which the State socialist or the Guild socialist recommends to us. It would, in fact, be easier to take the framework of the Co-operative Movement and adapt it to the control of the mining industry than to take the framework of the Miners' Federation or the Coal Controller's Office and adapt them.

It follows that the socialist, when he socializes any industry, should construct the machinery and organization for its control on the co-operative system. If he cannot or will not use the organization of the existing Movement, he should group his consumers in local and regional organs, federate them for national purposes, apply the system of local and national elected representatives, adopt the dividend on purchase. His industry will then be controlled by the community organized as consumers.

The multiplication of organs and machinery of government in society is an evil, and to leave the Co-operative Movement as it is and to create new organizations of the community of consumers to take over particular industries would involve this kind of complication and multiplication. I should much rather see the Movement developed and transformed into the organ of the community for the control of industry. But, if this is to be the ultimate function of the Movement, co-operators must consider its relation to two big questions which are now confronting them. Both these questions were dealt with by me to some extent from this point of view in *Co-operation and the Future of Industry*, but events have moved since that book was written, and it is, therefore, necessary to revise one's views of three years ago.

The reader will have gathered that my conception of the Movement is that it is the whole community of consumers in embryo and that it should be our object to transform it as rapidly as possible into the organ of the whole community of consumers. It would be fatal to do anything to identify the Movement with any section or class in the community. The class structure of society and class war are antagonistic to the whole principle and ideal of co-operation : it aims at abolishing economic competition and therefore the class distinctions which depend upon that economic competition. How does this affect the question of the Movement's entry into politics?

The Movement, as is well known, has already entered politics; there is a Co-operative Party financed by societies which runs candidates at elections and has already obtained some representation in the House of Commons; there are many ardent co-operators who would like to see societies and the Movement affiliated to the political Labour Party. The causes of this development were analyzed in my previous book, but, when I wrote it, although I saw and pointed out its possible dangers, I was inclined to accept it as inevitable. It is, I still think, probably inevitable. The Co-operative Movement is a non-capitalist industrial system in the midst of a capitalist system. The persecution of the Co-operative Movement during and since the war has opened the eyes of co-operators to the fact that capitalist interests are prepared, at the first opportunity, to use any powers which they may possess of controlling the law and the political machine to strike a blow at and, if possible, destroy the Movement. In these circumstances co-operators are necessarily driven to take the only course possible for their defence; if the capitalist strikes at them, as he is doing, through Parliament and the municipality, they must organize themselves politically and defend themselves in Parliament and the municipality. It is the old story of the trade unions over again : the capitalists struck at the unions through the law and thus drove trade unionists into politics. They are doing the same with the co-operators, and it is having precisely the same inevitable effects. And since the Movement is to-day a working-class movement, since its ideals are the ideals

of Labour, it is natural and right that, both within
and without the political field, it should work in close
co-operation with the other great Labour and Socialist
movements. But these facts should not blind co-
operators to the very real dangers of an entry
of their Movement into politics. A political party
cannot have a limited programme; it cannot
isolate industry and co-operation and send representatives to Parliament with a mandate confined
to these questions. It must have a general political
programme, for the co-operative representative does
not actually represent the Movement or even co-
operators, but a political constituency. You are a
co-operator because you are a consumer, and there
is no reason why every consumer should agree upon
the disestablishment of the Church or even upon
whether Englishmen are making the world safe for
democracy by shooting Irishmen and burning their
towns. It follows that when a society or the Movement enters politics or affiliates itself to a political
party, it may lose its claim to represent the whole
community of consumers.

The last question to be dealt with is one which I
treated at considerable length in my previous book,
the relation of the Movement to its employees. I
see no reason to alter or revise the main conclusions
arrived at there, namely, that what is wanted in
industry to-day is a kind of balance of power between
organized consumers and organized producers, and
that this could be attained by giving to the organizations of producers a recognized place and sphere within
the framework of the Movement. I wish, however,
briefly to relate this conclusion to the general
argument of this book. I have repeatedly argued in

these pages against the majority of socialist writers, whether orthodox Marxians, Communists, or Guild Socialists, that the ultimate basis of a socialist society should be consumption, and that the control of industry should ultimately be in the hands of the organized consumers. But my arguments applied to a fully developed socialist community in which a socialist psychology of consumption and production had already begun to operate. It does not apply to the transition period, and for this reason. If you oust the capitalist, you leave only two classes in the economic sphere, the consumer and the producer. Both these classes to-day are, as I have frequently repeated, permeated with the irrational and vicious psychology of consumption and production inherent in capitalism. By killing capitalism you would not kill this psychology, just as the guillotine which killed the king and the noble did not kill the psychology of 18th century oligarchy. If you expropriated the capitalist from any particular industry to-morrow, you would still find the producer in that industry and the consumer of its products acting in accordance with the capitalist psychology. If the consumer had the chance he would exploit the producer ; if the producer had the chance he would exploit the consumer. The Guild Socialist, the Syndicalist, and the Communist refuse to face this unpleasant truth, that the sins of society are visited upon the third and fourth genera-tion, and that you cannot make men good either by an Act of Parliament or by a revolution. But it is true, and that is the reason why it would be fatal to-day to give the control of industry completely into the hands of either the organized producers or the organized consumers.

I am aware that, by saying this, I shall alienate
many socialists, and that my critics and all those
who are hostile to socialism will cry in triumph that
I have given away my whole position. " You admit,"
they will say, " that, even if you destroy capitalism,
the psychology of capitalism will remain, in other
words, that what you object to in the capitalist and
his system is human nature." I have, of course, made
no such admission. What I say is that a century of
industrialized capitalism leaves every individual with
deep-seated and often unconscious beliefs and desires
implied in capitalism, and that no sudden revolution
or change in the framework of social organization will
extirpate those beliefs and desires. But they are not
inherent in human nature; they are not ineradicable.
Given an equitable distribution of wealth and power,
and a framework of social organizations and government which encourages co-operation and discourages
economic competition, and the " human nature " of
capitalism will become as obsolete and atrophied as
the " human nature " of cannibalism.

What the socialist should aim at in the immediate
future is the abolition of private ownership and
capitalist control, and the substitution of a partnership
between the organized consumers and producers. The
control must be shared between the Co-operative
Movement, developed and extended along the lines
traced in these pages, as the organ of the consumers,
and the trade unions or Guilds, as the organs of the
workers. It is, of course, easy to make this general
statement of principles; the real difficulty will occur
as soon as an attempt is made to apply it in detail,
to define the measure and sphere of control to be
assigned to each section and organization. I have

already reached the limits of space allowed to me in this book, and I cannot, therefore, enter into details; I can only indicate the more important points which the socialist should consider in seeking a solution.

Hitherto I have been looking at society and industry from the point of view of consumption and the consumer, for the very good reason that the object of industry is consumption and the ultimate basis of its organization and control should be the community of consumers. It is now necessary to look at industry from the point of view of the producer living in a semi-socialized world in which the control of industry is being transferred from the capitalist to the community of consumers. The producer will demand two things : protection against economic exploitation by the consumer and a certain measure of self-government. Both these demands are reasonable in the transition period. They have been most clearly and most forcibly stated by the Guild Socialists, and, while I think there is a certain amount of over-statement on their part, it seems to me that the co-operator can and must go a long way to meet their demand. So long as every consumer is not an industrial producer, there will always be a danger of economic exploitation of sections of the workers by consumers, if the control of industry is completely in the hands of the consumer's organizations. In the Co-operative Movement this exploitation would take the concrete form of low wages and a high dividend. The co-operative organization must make provision within its own framework for a recognition of the workers' organization as one of the parties which, together with itself, must arrive at a settlement of the remuneration of the producer. By

recognizing the trade unions and by accepting the
principle of a standard wage the Movement has gone
some way towards this end; but much more could
and should be done. Joint Boards for the settlement
of district and national rates should become part of
the recognized machinery of the Movement, with
Conciliation Boards, on which consumers' and producers' organizations have equal representation, for
final reference of a dispute which negotiation has failed
to settle. And if the workers show that they agree
with the contentions of the Guild Socialists with regard
to the wage system and begin seriously to transform
their trade unions into Guilds, the Movement can and
ought to accept the change. In that case the Guild
will be recognized as the producers' organization, and,
if it were fully developed, the consumers organized
in their societies or Movement, instead of paying
wages to the individual worker, would negotiate
directly with the Guild and settle, through the wages
board or conciliation board, the total remuneration
or, if the term be preferred, the share in the product
of industry which is to be taken by the Guild in return
for its services to the community of consumers. This
total remuneration or share will then be divided by
the Guild among its members in such proportion as
its members will themselves determine.

It will be seen that in this way, provided that both
the Guild and the co-operative systems develop fully,
the co-operator can meet and satisfy the demands of
the Guild Socialist with regard to the wage system.
There remains the much more difficult question of
the demand for self-government. It is obvious that,
if the worker be given full self-government in the
factory and in the general framework of industry, we

shall really have the whole of industry controlled by
the producer and his organization. If that is what
the Guild Socialist demands, no co-operator can admit
it, and his reasons have been given in the preceding
pages. But if the demand means that the worker
should be given a say in determining the conditions
under which he works and shall not be subject to
the autocratic control of an individual or class which
makes a profit out of his labour, then again the
co-operator can agree with the Guild Socialist.

It is easy to exaggerate and misstate this question
of self-government. Everyone, even the Guild
Socialist, agrees that in modern industry the large
majority of persons engaged in production must work
" under orders." Highly organized industry, depend-
ing upon complicated machinery, would be impossible
if every individual did his own work in his own time
and his own way. The real question is the origin and
object of the orders. What the worker legitimately
objects to is a social system under which these orders
are autocratically issued and the conditions under
which he works determined by a profit-making
individual or class, a system under which he can be
summarily dismissed, with no right of appeal to an
impartial tribunal, by a man who is at once legislator
and judge and plaintiff. But none of these objections
would hold good if the conditions under which the
producer worked and the general regulations for the
control of industry were jointly settled by the consumers organized in their societies and Movement and
the workers organized in their Guilds. The Movement
should, therefore, in my opinion, develop a system of
national and regional councils upon which societies
and trade unions or Guilds would have representation

and which would determine the general conditions under which production was carried on in the various trades and in industry as a whole.

The extreme Guild Socialist and anyone who accepts undiluted the producer's idea of socialism will dismiss me and my suggestions to that most terrible place of torment reserved for the renegade and bourgeois reformist. I am sorry, because I would much rather agree with a socialist than disagree with him. But it is only possible to go as far in social speculation as one's own brain is capable of carrying one. As against the capitalist and capitalism, I would go as far, probably, as the most extreme Guild Socialist or Red Communist in the demand for the emancipation of the worker. But socialism itself implies that what is true against capitalism and the capitalist is untrue against the community of consumers. My suggestions in the last few paragraphs will be seen to be all directed to establishing joint control and a balance of power within the framework of industry between the organized consumers and the organized producers. I believe that joint control and balance of power to be essential in the transition stage to pure socialism, for without it there will be exploitation of one class by the other and the growth of a rational psychology of consumption and production will be impossible. And, as a matter of fact, if the capitalist were eliminated, there would obviously be a far greater danger of the community of consumers being exploited by strong organizations of producers than of the consumers exploiting the organized producer. It will be a very long time before the Co-operative Movement has even a fraction of the power of exploitation which already resides in the Miners' Federation. So long as the psychology of capitalism remains, all power of exploitation is dangerous to the community, and in the transition period I wish to see it neither in the hands of the consumers nor co-operators, nor in the hands of the workers and producers. That is why I believe that the immediate object of the socialist should be to eliminate the capitalist and establish a balance of power between producer and consumer.

The National Labour Press, Ltd., Manchester and London.   32217

www.ingramcontent.com/pod-product-compliance
Lightning Source LLC
Chambersburg PA
CBHW070835100426
42813CB00003B/622